Vegan Breakfast Recipes

50+ Delicious Vegan Recipes, Quick & Easy To Make, Improve Your Health And Feel Amazing

GW00480950

not engaging in the rendering of legal, financial, medical or professional advice.

By reading this document, the reader agrees that under no circumstances are we responsible for any losses, direct or indirect, which are incurred as a result of the use of information contained within this document, including, but not limited to, —errors, omissions, or inaccuracies.

Table of Contents

Introduction

I want to thank you for choosing this book, "Vegan: Vegan breakfast recipes - 50 delicious vegan recipes, quick & easy to make, improve your health and feel amazing". Energy is not only an important concept in physics but it's also the driving force for all living things on this planet. Without energy, nothing can hope to survive. Food is the most primal source of energy, especially for human beings.

As Homo sapiens, and one of the largest consumers in any food chain, we are spoilt for choice when it comes to food on our plate. There are many food patterns, each varying with region, religion, health, preference etc. One of the most largely followed food patterns is the vegan lifestyle. Millions of people around the world often struggle with moral questions like "What am I doing to make a difference?" "What can I do to help animals and people?" "What can I do to grow on a personal level?" "What ethical choices can I make?"

Opting for a nutritious vegan diet can be an important answer to these questions. A vegan diet promotes abstinence from using animal products in your food in the spirit of rejecting the commodity status of animals. A vegan diet not only excludes the consumption of meat, fish or poultry but also excludes the consumption of food products obtained from animals like eggs, dairy products, honey etc.

A vegan diet is essentially made of plants, such as vegetables, fruits, grains and nuts. An overall balance of nutrients and vitamins in food is necessary for any human being, be it a growing child or an aging adult. The essential demand for calories, fat, proteins and minerals can be easily catered by a vegan food choice. A person following such a food pattern is often faced with a plethora of choices, which covers all the important points on the 'healthy checklist' and is merciful to the taste buds too.

Consumption of fruits and leafy vegetables supplies the basic need of a body for various vitamins. In addition to being rejuvenating to the mind, they provide the proper care to the body. There are loads of other foodstuff like whole grains, soy products, dried fruits that cater to the craving for delicious food and preserve the ethical standards you want your life to be based on. You can reply to the all those urges that motivate you to bind health and ethics in a carefully carved box called nutrition, with the confidence of a vegan diet.

In the course of this book, I have shared with you 50 delicious Vegan breakfast recipes, which will give your mornings the perfect kickstart.

Chapter 1:
Why Go Vegan?

Many a group of scientists argue that diets that include animal fat and animal protein can be detrimental to health. These are often high on cholesterol, which is the origin of innumerous coronary diseases. The excess consumption of fat in a non-vegan lifestyle leads to complications in an otherwise perfectly functioning body. People following a non-vegan diet are often found to be more prone to diseases like diabetes, high blood pressure, obesity, arthritis and even certain types of cancer. Some studies also indicate that vegan diets may even help in reversing the progression of certain diseases like prostate cancer.

A vegan diet is enriched in essential ingredients like dietary fiber, carbohydrates, magnesium, folic acid, vitamin A, vitamin C, vitamin E, iron and phytochemicals. A diet high in fiber helps fight against colon cancer and also promotes healthier bowel movement. Carbohydrates inclusion in daily meals means the body will have more energy to tackle the everyday tasks and trivialities. When you don't have enough carbs, your body will burn muscle tissue, which will severely hinder body development. Folic acid is rich in antioxidants, which not just prevents cell damage but also helps recover the body from it. Vitamin C is another antioxidant that helps keep the gums in your mouth healthy.

All those bruises and wounds that you might incur while coping with the pushed jump-starts and the rushed deadlines in life? They get healed faster due to the presence of abundant antioxidants in your body. Although popular belief states that a vegan diet may be insufficient when it comes to the supply of protein and calcium, this is often not true. Legumes like beans, peanuts and lentils are the best sources of protein for a vegan person. The inclusion of these in any diet can provide the extra boost of protein required for a healthy body.

There is also a wide variety when it comes to the supply for calcium, without which the human body is prone to diseases like osteoporosis. Against the famous myth that only meat can satisfy the need for calcium, plant milks such as those from hempseed, almonds, coconut make excellent options. These are not only fortified with calcium but even provide the essential fatty acids. A vegan lifestyle also helps cure any digestive disorders and abnormalities you might have. Preferring a vegan diet also means completely eliminating the risk of E. Coli infection, often caused due to the ingestion of contaminated animal products.

Vegan diet followers also exhibit charismatic features like an acne-free and clear skin. Other physical benefits include lower body mass index, which is often an indicator of healthy weight and the right amount of fat in a body, reduction in body odor, as the elimination of red meat and heavy dairy products indicates better digestion, healthier nails, lustrous hair and an alleviation of allergies often caused by consumption of animal products. In addition to the beneficiary aspect of a vegan diet, a vegan person also helps in shunning the modern practice of subjecting animals to cruelty in order to feed the human race.

Moreover, growing plants takes much fewer resources than growing animals on farms that often take a heavy toll on the environment. The small gain of catering to your salivating tongue is often won out by the much larger and urgent need for survival of animal life on this planet. That is the essence of a vegan diet. To fulfill the ethical duty of being a human being while simultaneously enjoying the nutritious boosts provided by the food on your plate.

Protein Meal Plan

Going vegan means strictly going meatless and of course not eating anything that is animal based. However, going off animal products does not mean that you should forgo all the nutrition that you get from animal products. You should make sure that your body gets enough of proteins, to remain strong and healthy. Do you think it is difficult to get proteins if you are not a meat eater? No, not at all, that is one of the biggest myths. One can get sufficient proteins from plant sources.

How much protein does our body require? It needs about 0.8 grams protein for every kilogram we weigh. Almost all plant based food like vegetables, grains, nuts, pulses, etc. contain protein. So a male who weighs around 70 kgs or 154 pounds would need 63 grams of protein in a vegan diet and a female who weighs around 58 kgs or 126 pounds would need 52 grams of protein.

Some of the plant based food that contains protein are all types of beans and lentils, soybean and its products like soymilk, tofu, tempeh, soy cheese, soy yogurt etc., nuts like almonds, walnuts, peanuts, pecans, hazelnuts etc., seeds like pumpkin seeds, sunflower seeds, chia seeds etc., grains like quinoa, wheat, rice, oats barley, millet etc. The proteins from these foods are sufficient for those who are on a vegan diet. So it is recommended that you eat a variety of foods so that you get the proteins required for your body.

A typical High protein breakfast meal plan:

1. Any of the recipes mentioned in the chapter High protein breakfast recipes

2. A cup of non-dairy milk like soymilk, almond milk or coconut milk or any smoothies or non-dairy yogurt.

3. A serving of fruits like pear, cantaloupe, berries, apple, banana etc.

Weight Loss Meal Plan

For you to lose weight you need to opt for a low carb diet. Do not completely omit carbohydrates from your diet. You need to eat a lot of fiber rich food. Eat whole grains, vegetables especially green leafy vegetables, fruits, nuts, and legumes etc.

One should have at least 6 servings (1/2 cup each) of grains, 3 servings of legumes, 4 servings of vegetables out of which at least one serving should be raw food in the form of salads and 3 servings of fruits in a day.

Drink lots of water. Drink at least 6 to 8 glasses of water in a day.

Do not drink fruit juices. Cut down on sugar, junk food, aerated drinks, sweets etc. Avoid saturated fat and use vegetable oils to the minimum possible. Avoid fattening salad dressings.

Start exercising regularly. Exercise for at least 4 days a week. You can exercise at home or the gym, practice yoga or simply go for walks.

A typical Weight Loss Breakfast meal plan

1. Any breakfast recipe of your choice that contains vegetables and proteins.

2. A smoothie or a cup of non-dairy milk like soymilk, coconut milk, almond milk, etc.

3. A serving of fruits

4. A serving of grains

5. A serving of legumes

Try to vary the foods you choose every day. For e.g. If you have berries for fruit one day, have something else the next day. The same goes with grains and legumes too. If you have smoothie one day, have non-dairy milk on the next day or some other smoothie. Try to choose your fruits such that they are high on nutrition and low on calories.

Chapter 2:
Protein Contents of Commonly Used Vegan Foods

Once you know the protein contents of different vegan foods, it is easier for you to decide the food that is right for you to eat and what is not.

- A cup of tempeh has 31 grams of protein.

- A cup of cooked soybeans has 29 grams of protein.

- A cup of cooked textured vegetable protein has 16 grams of protein.

- A cup of cooked bulgur or buckwheat or whole wheat couscous has 6 grams of protein.

- A cup of cooked spinach has 5 grams of protein.

- A cup of cooked kale has 4.5 grams of protein.

- A cup of baked beans has 12 grams of protein.

- A cup of instant oatmeal has 6 grams of protein.

- A cup of plain soymilk has 7 grams of protein.

- A cup of cooked brown rice has 5 grams of protein.

- A cup of oyster mushrooms has 5 grams of protein.

- A cup of cooked lentils has 18 grams of protein.

- A cup of cooked cannellini beans or cranberry beans has 17 grams of protein.

- A cup of cooked millets has 8.4 grams of protein.

- A cup of cooked oat bran or wild rice or rye berries has 7 grams of protein.

- A cup of cooked split peas or navy beans has 16 grams of protein.

- A cup of cooked chickpeas or kidney beans or lima beans or pinto beans or black beans or Great Northern beans or Anasazi has 15 grams of protein.

- A cup of cooked black-eyed peas or mung beans has 13 grams of protein.

- A cup of broccoli or Brussels sprouts or a medium artichoke has 4 grams of protein.

- A cup of cooked peas or quinoa or spaghetti or pasta has 8 grams of protein.

- Half a cup of cooked edamame has 15 grams of protein.

- Half a cup of almonds has 11 grams of protein.

- Half a cup of sunflower seeds has 12 grams of protein.

- Half a cup of cashews has 10 grams of protein.

- A quarter of a cup of chia seeds has 12 grams of protein.

- A quarter of a cup of hemp seeds has 10 grams of protein.

- A quarter of a cup of flax seeds has 8 grams of protein.

- A quarter of a cup of chia seeds has 12 grams of protein.

- A quarter of a cup of walnuts or hazelnuts or Brazil nuts has 5 grams of protein.

- A quarter of a cup of pine nuts has 4 grams of protein.

- A quarter of a cup of chia pistachio nuts has 6 grams of protein.

- A quarter of a cup of sesame seeds has 7 grams of protein.

- 3 ounces seitan has 21 grams of protein

- 4 ounces firm tofu has 11 grams of protein

- 4 ounces regular tofu has 10 grams of protein

- 8 ounces plain soy yogurt has 6 grams of protein

- 1 medium bagel has 10 grams of protein

- 2 slice of whole wheat bread has 7 grams of protein

- 2 tablespoons of wheat germ has 4 grams of protein

- 2 tablespoons of almond butter has 7 grams of protein

- 2 tablespoons of peanut butter has 8 grams of protein

Chapter 3:
Tasty And Healthy Breakfast Recipes

Quinoa With Strawberries And Banana

Ingredients:

- ½ cup of quinoa

- ½ cup of strawberries

- 1 small banana

- 11/2 cups of coconut milk

- 1 cup water

- 2 tablespoons of toasted coconut

- 2 tablespoons of toasted almonds

- ½ teaspoon powdered cinnamon

- 1 teaspoon vanilla

Instructions:

1. Let us begin with preparing the quinoa. The most important aspect of cooking any dish with quinoa is to rinse it well in order to remove the bitter brackish taste completely. The thumb rule here is the 1:2 ratio, i.e., 2 parts of water for 1 part quinoa. Rinse the quinoa well.

2. Now take the rinsed quinoa in a saucepan and add the water. Bring it to a boil over a high flame.

3. Now it is time to add the cinnamon and vanilla. As soon as you do add them, reduce the heat and let the mixture simmer for about 15 minutes while the pan remains covered.

4. One this is done, take the pan off the heat and let it stand for another 10 minutes while the mixture cools down. At the same time, fluff the contents softly with a fork.

5. Make sure that you slice the banana, strawberries and nuts into small chunks.

6. You are ready to serve now. Divide the mixture equally into smaller bowls and add the coconut milk along with the banana, strawberries and nuts.

Raw Parfaits

Ingredients:

- 1 cup almonds

- 1 cup walnuts

- ½ cup pumpkin seeds

- 1 cup cashews

- 1/3 cup water

- ¼ cup flax seeds

- ¼ cup chia seeds

- ¼ teaspoon cinnamon

- ¼ teaspoon vanilla

- 11/2 tablespoon agave

- ¼ teaspoon salt

- Half a cup of strawberries or blackberries

Instructions:

1. Parfaits are hands down one of the most delicious, healthy and easy to make breakfast dishes that are packed with nutrients and vitamins. So let us look into how we can make one.

2. First of all, make sure that the cashew nuts are well soaked (for at least 2 hours).

3. Now take a food processor and add all the seeds and nuts into it. Process the contents for a few seconds. Note that we want small chunks and not a fine powder, so keep an eye on the processor.

4. Let us make the cashew cream next. Add the soaked nuts into a blender, pour in a little amount of water and blend the contents into a fine paste.

5. Take the container and make a layer of berries in the bottom. On top of that, add the flax and chia seeds. Spread a layer of cashew cream and then more nuts.

6. Finally on top of everything add the rest of the fruits.

Sweet Potato Burritos With Black Beans

Ingredients:

- 1 medium sized sweet potato

- 1 (1 pound) can of black beans

- 4 tortillas of medium size

- 8 mushrooms

- 3 green onions

- 2 teaspoon cumin

- A few green chilies

- 2 cups of spinach

- 1 pound of tofu

- 1 tablespoon nutritional yeast

- 4 tablespoons of olive oil

- Salt and pepper to preference

Instructions:

1. Begin with preheating the oven to a temperature of 375 degree Celsius.

2. Now let us bake the potatoes. Place them on a sheet that has been rubbed with some olive oil. Sprinkle with potatoes with the salt and pepper. Bake them for

approximately half an hour or until the potatoes are tender.

3. While the potatoes are baking, let us do the rest of the cooking. Add the balance olive oil into a pan and add the mushrooms and onions for a few minutes.

4. Next goes in the tofu, chilies, cumin and yeast. And once the tofu gets a bit warm, add the spinach. The mixture should be cooked till the spinach is done, then keep it aside.

5. In the same pan, heat the beans.

6. Once everything is cooked, wrap the mixture in the tortillas.

Vegan French Toast

Ingredients:

- 6 slices of your favored type of bread

- 2 tablespoon millet flour

- 1 teaspoon cinnamon

- 2 tablespoon maple syrup

- 1 cup almond milk

- 1 tablespoon nutritional yeast

- A little amount of ground nutmeg

- 11/2 teaspoon coconut oil

- A pinch of salt

Instructions:

1. Take a bowl and mix together the almond milk, maple syrup, yeast, nutmeg, salt and cinnamon along with the flour.

2. Now place the bread slices in a flat dish and slather the mixture evenly on one side, flip over and then continue on the other side.

3. Take a flat-bottomed pan and heat the coconut oil on a medium flame. Once sufficiently hot, place the bread slices and cook for a few minutes until they gain a golden hue.

4. You can serve with a bit of maple syrup rubbed on the slices.

Vegan Omelet

Ingredients:

- A quarter pound of firm tofu

- ½ cup of soy milk

- 1 tablespoon cornstarch

- A pinch of cayenne pepper

- 1 tablespoon brown rice flour

- A pinch of turmeric

- ¼ teaspoon salt

- A medium sized onion

- Half an avocado

Instructions:

1. As is usually done with tofu, place the slab on a few sheet of tissue paper while pressing down on it to squeeze out all the water. After this, slice the tofu into medium sized chunks.

2. Now put all the ingredients including the tofu into a food processor and blend it into smooth thick consistency. Check and add enough soymilk in order to ensure that the batter flows.

3. Now heat a pan and sauté the onions. Once they are done, take them off the pan and mix the avocado pieces.

4. Now pour the batter onto the pan and cook it becomes fluffy.

5. Once the "omelet" is ready, fold it and stuff it with the onion and avocado filling. You are ready to go.

Basic Cinnamon Rolls

Ingredients:

- 4 cups of wheat flour

- 12 tablespoons of vegan butter

- 1 cup of almond milk

- 1/3 cup orange juice

- 2 tablespoon baking powder

- 1 teaspoon vanilla extract

- 3 teaspoon baking soda

- 1 cup of brown sugar

- 1 teaspoon salt

- ½ teaspoon cinnamon

- 2 tablespoon organic raisins

Instructions:

1. Let us begin by preheating the oven to a temperature of 375 degree Celsius.

2. Take a bowl and mix in all the dry and wet ingredients in order to form soft dough. Every now and then add some more almond milk to ensure that the dough is pliable and soft.

3. Now take a board and sprinkle some flour on it. Roll out the dough in a flat rectangle shape about 1 inch thick.

4. Once the dough is flattened out, brush a layer of vegan butter and a few drops of vanilla on top. Over that, sprinkle the cinnamon powder, raisins and a generous helping of brown sugar.

5. Now roll the sheet of dough from one end, completely till the next, so that a tube is formed.

6. Cut the roll into pieces, which are 11/2 inch long and bake them for half an hour and you are good to go.

Pop Tarts

Ingredients:

- 1/2 cup of wheat four

- 11/2 tablespoon maple syrup

- 2 tablespoon coconut oil

- ¾ teaspoon vanilla extract

- ¼ teaspoon salt

- 3 or strawberries

- 1 banana

Instructions:

1. As in the case of any baking dish, let us begin by preheating the oven; in this case to 350 degree Celsius.

2. Take a bowl and mix together all the dry and wet ingredients. Knead the dough nicely and transfer the mixture onto a flat board. Sprinkle some dough on the board and cut up the dough into flat square pieces.

3. Transfer the slices into a bag and place in the refrigerator. Make sure that the bag remains in the fridge for at least 20 minutes. This is to avoid crumbling of the tarts.

4. Chop the strawberries and banana into really small pieces.

5. Grease a baking pan and spread out the rectangle pieces. On half the pieces, spread the sliced fruits and place the balance pieces on top. Bake for 15 minutes and you are good to go.

Cinnamon Toast Crunch

Ingredients:

- 1 cup chickpea flour

- 2 teaspoon cinnamon

- 1 teaspoon vanilla extract

- 2 tablespoon applesauce

- ¾ cup water

- ¼ teaspoon salt

- 3 cup almond milk

- Sugar to taste

Instructions:

1. Let us start by preheating the oven to 200 degree Celsius.

2. Take a bowl and mix together the flour, 1 teaspoon cinnamon, applesauce, vanilla extract, salt and sugar to taste. Finally add the water and beat it into dough. Make sure that the mixture is smooth and fine.

3. Now take a cookie sheet and pour the batter into it.

4. Sprinkle the rest of the cinnamon directly on top of the batter.

5. Bake for half an hour and cut the cereal into 1-inch squares.

6. Now dunk the pieces into the bowl of almond milk and you are ready to savor one of the most delicious toast crunches ever.

Oatmeal With Blueberries

Ingredients:

- 11/2 cups of Irish oats

- 1 small carton of Blueberries.

- 2 cups of coconut milk

- 1/3 cup brown sugar

- 2 cups water

- 1 cup of honey

- A pinch of salt

Instructions:

1. Take a saucepan and mix in all the ingredients except the honey and blueberries and heat it over a flame.

2. Once it starts boiling, reduce the heat and let it simmer for about 20 minutes until the mixture is really thick.

3. Now transfer the contents into a baking dish and let it cool down in room temperature for an hour. This will allow the oatmeal to turn into a cake like consistency.

4. While the oatmeal is cooling down, let us poach the blueberries in honey.

5. Take a saucepan and heat the honey till it boils. Now pour it over the blueberries.

6. Meanwhile, after emptying the pan, place the oatmeal on the pan and sear it on both sides.

7. Now place it on a dish and scoop the poached blueberries on top of it.

Chickpea pancakes

Ingredients:

- ½ cup of chickpea flour

- ¼ cup of red pepper (chopped)

- 1 green onion (chopped)

- 1 avocado

- A pinch of pepper flakes

- ¼ teaspoon garlic powder

- ¼ teaspoon baking powder

- ¼ teaspoon sea salt

- 1/8 teaspoon black pepper (ground)

- 1 cup water

- Olive oil for cooking

Instructions:

1. Take a small bowl and mix together the garlic, baking powder, salt, pepper and the chickpea flour along with the water. Whisk the contents into a smooth batter devoid of bubbles.

2. Mix in the onion and avocado and stir the contents well.

3. Heat a skillet over medium flame and pour in some olive oil.

4. When the oil is heated, pour the desired amount of the batter in a round shape and cook it, flipping it over after 3 or 4 minutes.

Blueberry Banana Bars

Ingredients:

- 1 cup dates (seedless and halved)

- 1 large banana

- 1 cup blueberries

- ½ cup walnuts

- 3 cups oats

- 11/2 tablespoon baking powder

- ¼ teaspoon nutmeg

- ¾ teaspoon cinnamon (ground)

- 11/2 cups apple juice

- 1 teaspoon vanilla extract

Instructions:

1. Before we begin, preheat the oven to 200 degree Celsius and at the same time, soak the dates in the apple juice for about 15 minutes.

2. Take a bowl and mix together the nutmeg, cinnamon, baking powder and 2 cups of the oats.

3. Now add the banana and the rest of the oats into a blender along with the vanilla extract. Top it off with the apple juice that has been drained. Blend the mixture

until the contents are creamy. Finally add the dates and blend it for a second more.

4. Transfer this mixture into the dry bowl and add the blueberries and walnuts.

5. Pour the entire mixture into the baking dish and bake for half an hour.

Tofu Zucchini Scrambled

Ingredients:

- 1 tablespoon vegan butter

- 1 pack of tofu (firm)

- 2 Zucchini (chopped)

- ¼ cup basil (shredded)

- ½ cup onion (finely diced)

- 1 clove garlic

- ½ teaspoon turmeric

- Black salt and pepper to taste

Instructions:

1. Take a skillet and heat it over a medium flame.

2. Add the Zucchini and onions along with the garlic and butter to the skillet for a few minutes until the onion are slightly brown and the zucchini becomes a little crispy.

3. Now add the tofu after crumbling it thoroughly. Add the turmeric, salt and pepper for taste. After cooking for 5 minutes, add the basil.

Biscuits And Gravy

Ingredients:

- 21/2 cups flour

- 31/2 cups soy milk

- 1 tablespoon baking powder

- 4 tablespoons vegan butter

- I tablespoon lemon juice

- ½ teaspoon baking soda

- ¾ teaspoon salt and pepper

- Vegan breakfast sausage

- Red pepper (crushed)

- Half a jalapeno (minced)

- 1 small onion (diced)

Instructions:

1. Let us start by heating the oven to 450 degree Celsius.

2. Take a large bowl and mix together the flour, butter, baking powder, salt and the baking soda. Add soymilk into the mixture, little by little, and keep stirring until soft dough is formed.

3. Now on a board, sprinkle some flour and spread out the dough about a quarter of an inch thick so that you can cut out biscuit shaped circles.

4. After doing so, smear the biscuits with olive oil and bake them for 15 minutes.

5. Meanwhile we can work on that gravy. In a saucepan, the onions, sausages and jalapenos have to be sautéed in olive oil over medium heat. About 10 minutes later, the rest of the milk along with the flour and spices can be added till the desired consistency is achieved.

6. Once the biscuits and gravy are done, you can have the top the biscuits with the gravy and serve.

Coconut Blueberry Muffins

Ingredients:

- 2 cups flour

- 3 tablespoons shredded coconut

- 1 cup blueberries

- 3 teaspoons baking powder

- ½ cup virgin coconut oil

- ½ cup almond milk

- ½ cup maple syrup

- 1 tablespoon flax seeds (ground)

- ¼ teaspoon vanilla extract

- 1 large banana

- 2 tablespoons lemon juice

- ¾ teaspoon salt

- Sugar to taste

Instructions:

1. As usual, let us begin by preheating the oven to a temperature of 375 degree Celsius. Next, in a large bowl, mix the flour, flax seeds, baking powder and salt.

2. In another bowl, combine the coconut oil and almond milk along with sugar to taste. Now mix this with the flour bowl along with the banana, shredded coconut, vanilla, and lemon and at last the blueberries.

3. Transfer the mixture to muffin molds and bake for 20 minutes.

Chocolate Covered Doughnuts

Ingredients:

- ½ cup flour

- ¼ cup potato starch

- 2 teaspoon baking powder

- ½ cup brown rice flour

- ¼ cup arrowroot powder

- ½ tablespoon apple cider vinegar

- ½ cup almond or soy milk

- 11/2 teaspoon Ener-G egg replacer

- ½ teaspoon vanilla extract

- Vegan Chocolate icing

- ¼ cup oil

- ¼ teaspoon salt

Instructions:

1. Pre heat the oven to 350 degree Celsius.

2. Take a bowl and mix together all the ingredients, leaving aside a little oil.

3. Once mixed well, the mixture should be transferred into a zip-lock bag. After this, grease the baking pan.

4. Cut a corner off the bag and use that to squirt the batter in round shape onto the pan.

5. Bake for 8 minutes and then apply the chocolate icing once the doughnuts are cool enough.

Coconut "Yogurt"

Ingredients:

- 2 cups coconut meat

- ½ cup coconut water

- Sugar to taste

- ½ teaspoon pro-biotic powder

- 1 tablespoon lemon juice

- A pinch of salt

- 2 teaspoons chia seeds

Instructions:

1. Mix all the ingredients except the chia seeds in a bowl and transfer the contents into a blender. Keep blending until you get a very smooth mixture, all the while adding the desired amount of sugar.

2. Now place the container in a fridge so as to let it cool down.

3. Bow you have the "yogurt". It can either be taken in jars like parfait, or can be taken just like that in a dish. In both the cases, the chia seeds can be used to garnish.

Breakfast Tacos

Ingredients:

- ½ pound firm tofu

- Tortillas as per your requirement

- ¼ cup pomegranate arils

- 1 cup of black beans

- 1 cup cilantro

- 1 avocado (sliced)

- 1 lemon

- ¼ medium sized onion

- ¾ teaspoon garlic powder

- 1 teaspoon cumin

- ½ teaspoon chili powder

- 1 tablespoon salsa

- 1 tablespoon water

- 3A pinch of salt

Instructions:

1. As usual, squeeze the tofu by placing it on a bunch of tissue papers and weighing down on it

2. Cook the black beans in a small saucepan over medium heat after adding a pinch each of the cumin, garlic, salt and chili powder.

3. Next make the sauce by adding the rest of the dry spices and salsa along with water to a small bowl.

4. Take a medium sized skillet and heat some oil it. Add the tofu and cook till it turns brown. Add the seasoning and continue the cooking for another 10 minutes.

5. Stuff the tortilla with the beans, onions, and avocadoes and salsa with the rest of the seasoning and you are ready to serve.

Tofu Avocado Benedict

Ingredients:

- 1 English muffin
- 1 pound tofu
- ½ an avocado
- Handful of lettuce
- 2 tablespoon canola oil
- 2 slices of tomato
- 2 tablespoon of vegan butter
- 1 tablespoon nutritional yeast
- 2-3 teaspoon lemon juice
- Pinch of pepper
- 1 tablespoon flour
- ½ cup of almond milk or soy milk

Instructions:

1. Let us begin with the preparation of the sauce. Take a small saucepan and heat it while adding the flour and milk slowly. Keep stirring and let it boil for a few minutes.

2. Take the pan away from the heat and add the lemon, yeast and the rest of the seasoning.

3. Now it's the tofu and the rest of the dish. Slice them into ½ inch thick pieces and sprinkle a bit of salt and pepper on both sides. Next fry them lightly in the canola oil.

4. Assemble the dish by slicing the muffin into two and toasting it. Then place a little lettuce, a slice of tomato and a piece of tofu all slathered generously with the sauce.

Banana Bead Smoothie

Ingredients:

- I banana (medium sized to large and frozen)
- 1 tablespoon walnuts (raw)
- 1/3 cup Quinoa
- ½ teaspoon vanilla extract
- Ground cinnamon
- 1 cup water
- 1 date (pitted)
- 2 teaspoon flax oil
- A pinch of allspice

Instructions:

1. Before you begin the actual blending of the smoothie ingredients, make sure that the quinoa is cooked really well. You can even make use of buckwheat in place of the quinoa if you do not have access to it.

2. Once the quinoa is cooked and sufficiently cool, add all the ingredients into the blender. You will have to blend them for a good half a minute or more to achieve a smooth consistency.

3. Next pour into a glass and top if off with some extra walnuts and cinnamon.

Apple Pie Smoothie

Ingredients:

- 1 medium to large sized apple

- ½ English cucumber

- ¼ avocado

- 2 cups spinach

- ½ apple juice (unsweetened)

- 1 tablespoon walnuts

- ¼ teaspoon vanilla extract

- A pinch of nutmeg (ground)

- ½ teaspoon cinnamon (ground)

- Some ice cubes (5 or 6)

Instructions:

1. Before we begin, let us deal with the fruits first. The apple and avocado have to be chopped first and then frozen well. So plan for this smoothie in advance and make sure that the freezing is done.

2. Next, add all the ingredients, including the apples and avocadoes into the blender and blend well for a minimum of 30 seconds. You can continue blending for a little longer if you like you smoothie to be creamy.

Strawberry Cheesecake Smoothie

Ingredients:

- 1 cup of strawberries

- 3 tablespoon oats

- 1 tablespoon cashew nuts

- 1 cup of almond milk

- 1 teaspoon vinegar

- ½ teaspoon vanilla

- 1 teaspoon lemon juice

- 1 tablespoon chia seed

Instructions

1. Compared to the other smoothies, this one has a slight difference. In order to bring out the true essence of this smoothie, you have to mix all the ingredients in a jar and refrigerate it overnight.

2. In the morning, transfer the contents to a blender and process it for as much time it takes to fetch you a smoothie with creamy smooth consistency.

Full Green Smoothie

Ingredients:

- 1 cup of organic Green tea

- 3 cups of spinach

- 2 cups honeydew melon

- 1 cucumber

- ½ inch ginger root

- 1 teaspoon lemon juice

Instructions:

1. As always, the fruits have to be sliced and diced first. In this case, the cucumber should be sliced into medium sized pieces after taking out the seeds.

2. Next the honeydew melon should be cut into cube shapes.

3. After this, throw in everything into the blender and process for a good half a minute. You can continue for a longer duration if a creamier smoothie is desired.

Mint Chocolate Smoothie

Ingredients:

- 1 peppermint tea bag

- 3 tablespoons of chocolate chips made from a non-diary source

- 1 banana (medium sized and frozen beforehand)

- 1 cup almond milk or soy milk (unsweetened)

- 2 cups spinach

- 2 tablespoons hemp hearts

- ½ cup boiling water

- 5 to 6 ice cubes

Instructions:

1. Before you get started, please note that this is one smoothie that has to be prepared and kept at least half an hour before consumption.

2. Let us focus on the tea first. Dunk and steep the tea bag in the cup of boiling water for some time so that all the flour comes out concentrated. Then you have to let it stand and cool down so that it is fit to use in the smoothie. Strictly speaking, this should take only half an hour but in my experience, the mint flavor becomes stronger and more balanced when you let the cup stand overnight.

3. You now have to merely add in all the ingredients except the chocolate chips into the blender and process for a good 30 seconds.

4. After this, drop three fourths of the chocolate chips on the top and stir it in.

5. Use the rest to garnish when you serve the smoothie.

Cranberry & Ruby Grapefruit Compote

Makes: 6 servings of 1/2 cup each

Ingredients:

- 1 cup fresh or frozen cranberries

- 1 1/2 large red grapefruit, peel, deseed, separate segments and remove membrane

- 10 tablespoons water

- 1 inch piece cinnamon stick

- 4-5 thin strips orange zest

- 1/4 cup orange juice

- 1/4 cup sugar

- A few fresh mint sprigs to garnish

Instructions:

1. Add all the ingredients except grapefruit to a saucepan. Place the saucepan over medium high heat. Cook until the cranberries are tender.

2. Remove from heat. Transfer into a bowl and chill for at least 2 hours.

3. Remove the bowl from the refrigerator. Add the grapefruits to it. Mix well.

4. Serve in individual bowls, garnished with mint sprigs. Refrigerate until use. It can last for 2 days if refrigerated.

Spinach Artichoke Pizza:

Makes: 4 servings

Ingredients:

- 1/2 pound prepared pizza dough
- 1/2 cup spinach, chopped
- 1/2 cup artichoke hearts, chopped
- 1/4 cup pesto
- 1/2 cup vegan mozzarella cheese
- 1/4 cup vegan parmesan cheese

Instructions:

1. Dust your work area with a little flour. Place the pizza flour over it and roll into a round pizza with a rolling pin.

2. Gently transfer the rolled dough into a pizza pan.

3. Spread pesto over the pizza. Sprinkle artichoke hearts and spinach all over the pizza.

4. Finally sprinkle the cheese over it.

5. Bake in a preheated oven at 450 degree F for about 18-20 minutes or until the cheese is melted and light brown.

6. Remove from the oven. Cool slightly. Slice into 4 wedges and serve immediately.1234567890

No Bake Cinnamon Rolls:

Makes: 4 servings

Ingredients:

For Cinnamon rolls

- 3 cups dates, pitted
- 1 cup old fashioned oats
- 4 tablespoons coconut oil
- 5-6 tablespoons warm water
- 5-6 tablespoons flour
- 1 teaspoon vanilla extract

For the Icing:

- 2 cups cashews, soaked
- 1 1/2 cups water
- 24 teaspoons pure maple syrup
- 2 teaspoons ground cinnamon

Instructions:

1. For the cinnamon rolls: Add dates, oats, cinnamon, oil and vanilla to the food processor and pulse. Add about a tablespoon of water at a time and continue pulsing until the mixture is well combined. Remove and divide into 4 balls.

2. Spread a little flour on your work area. Place one ball of the date's mixture over the flour. Use a rolling pin and roll the mixture into a thin 1-inch wide strip. Twist the rolled strip to form a roll.

3. Repeat step 2 with the remaining 3 balls of the mixture.

4. To make the icing: Blend together all the ingredients of the icing. Spread over the roll.

5. Serve as it is or slightly warm it in the microwave and serve.

Avocado Mousse:

Serves: 4

Ingredients:

- 2 ripe avocados, peeled, pitted, chopped

- 2 cups young coconut flesh

- A little coconut water if required

- Cacao nibs for garnishing (optional)

Instructions:

1. Blend together avocado and coconut flesh in a blender until smooth. Add coconut water if it is too thick and blend until smooth.

2. Pour into 4 glasses. Garnish with cacao nibs and serve.

Roasted Chickpea and Broccoli Burrito

Makes: 4 servings

Ingredients:

- 1 can (15 ounce) unsalted chickpeas, rinsed, drained
- 1 1/2 tablespoons olive oil
- 1 medium onion, chopped
- 2 cloves garlic, minced
- 1/2 pound broccoli, chopped
- 1 medium red bell pepper, chopped
- 1 tablespoon low sodium soy sauce
- 1/2 teaspoon ground cumin
- 1/4 teaspoon ground coriander
- 1 teaspoon chili powder
- 1/2 teaspoon smoked paprika
- Cayenne pepper to taste
- 4 tortillas (8 inches each)
- Juice of a lime

Instructions:

1. Add all the ingredients to a bowl except garlic, tortillas and lime juice. Mix well.

2. Transfer on to a rimmed baking sheet. Bake in a preheated oven at 425 degree F for 20 minutes.

3. Add garlic and bake for 15 minutes. Remove from the oven.

4. Add lemon juice and mix well. Divide and place over the tortillas. Roll up and serve.

Vegan Granola Bars:

Makes: 4 servings

Ingredients:

- 1/2 cup dates, pitted, soaked in cold water for a while

- 3/4 cup old fashioned oats, finely ground

- 1 tablespoon oat bran

- 1/4 cup pecans, toasted, finely ground

- 1/4 cup pecans, toasted, roughly chopped

- 1/4 cup macadamia nuts, unsalted, toasted, finely ground

- 1/4 cup macadamia nuts, unsalted, toasted, finely ground

- 3 tablespoons dried cherries, chopped

- 3 tablespoons dried papaya, cut into 1/2 inch pieces

- 3 tablespoons dried blueberries

- 1 tablespoon wheat germ

- 1 1/2 tablespoons ground flaxseeds

- 1/4 teaspoon coarse salt

- 1 1/2 tablespoon honey

- 1/4 teaspoon ground cinnamon

- Cooking spray

Instructions:

1. Place the soaked dates in a small saucepan with enough water to just cover the dates. Bring to a boil.

2. Drain and when cooled slightly, blend in a blender until smooth.

3. Mix together in a bowl, oats, pecans, macadamia nuts, papaya, cherries, blueberries, bran, flaxseed, wheat germ, salt and cinnamon. Pour honey and the pureed dates over it. Mix well.

4. Spray a baking dish with cooking spray. Transfer the whole mixture into the dish. Press the mixture well into the pan.

5. Bake in a preheated oven at 350 degree F until golden brown.

6. Remove from the oven and place the dish on a wire rack. Slice into 4 bars and serve. 1234567890

Breakfast Parfait Bombs:

Makes: 4 servings

Ingredients:

For nut mix:

- 1/2 cup walnuts

- 1/2 cup almonds

- 1/4 cup flax meal

- 1/4 cup sunflower seeds

- 1/4 cup pumpkin seeds

- 2 - 3 tablespoons shredded coconut (optional)

- Sweetener to taste (optional)

For vanilla cashew cream:

- 1/2 cup cashews, soaked in water for 2 hours

- 1 tablespoon agave nectar

- 2 to 4 tablespoons water

- A pinch Celtic sea salt

- 1/4 teaspoon vanilla extract

To serve:

- 1/2 cup blueberries

- 1/2 cup raspberries

Instructions:

1. To make the nut mix: Place all the ingredients of the nut mix in the food processor and pulse for a couple of seconds so that the nuts and seeds are coarse. Do not grind it too fine. Add shredded coconut and sweetener if using.

2. Transfer into a bowl.

3. To make vanilla cashew cream: Blend together all the ingredients until smooth. Remove and transfer into a bowl.

4. To serve: Take 4 medium sized glasses. Place a few blueberries in each of the glasses. Next place raspberries over the blueberries.

5. Next place some nut mix over the raspberries. Add about a spoonful of the vanilla cashew cream. Repeat this layer once more.

6. For the last layers, first place some blueberries over the cashew cream and finally top with raspberries.

7. Refrigerate if you like it chilled or else serve it as it is.

Raw Buckwheat, Apple, Walnut Porridge:

Makes: 4 servings

Ingredients:

- 2 cups raw buckwheat, hulled, soaked in water preferably overnight

- 2 cups walnuts, soaked in water, preferably overnight

- 4 green apples, cored, chopped

- Juice of 2 oranges

- 1 teaspoon vanilla extract

- 1 teaspoon ground cardamom

- 1/2 cup pomegranate seeds

- 1 cup berries of your choice

Instructions:

1. Rinse and drain the buckwheat and walnuts. Add buckwheat, walnuts, apple, vanilla extract, and cardamom to the food processor. Blend until smooth.

2. Transfer into 4 individual serving bowls. Place pomegranate and berries on top and serve. If you like it chilled, refrigerate for a while and serve. This can last for 3-4 days if refrigerated.

3. Note: You can top with anything else you like.

Quick Oats Upma:

Makes: 6 servings

Ingredients:

- 4 cups quick cooking oats
- 2 large onions, finely chopped
- 4 medium carrots, peeled, diced
- 2 cups bell pepper, diced
- 3 cups water
- 1 1/2 teaspoon cumin seeds
- 2 1/2 tablespoons vegetable oil, divided
- Juice of a lemon
- Salt to taste
- 2-3 green chilies, slit
- 2 tablespoons fresh cilantro, chopped

Instructions:

1. Place a heavy bottomed pan over medium low heat. Add half the oil. When the oil is heated, add oats and roast it until the oats begin to turn light brown.

2. Transfer the oats into a bowl and set it aside.

3. Place the pan back on medium low heat. Add the remaining oil. When oil is hot, add cumin seeds. When the seeds sizzle, add onions and green chilies. Sauté until the onions are translucent.

4. Add carrots and bell pepper. Sprinkle some water and cook until the carrots are soft.

5. Add salt and oats. Stir for a few seconds and add water. Mix well.

6. Cook until all the water is absorbed. Add lemon juice and mix well.

7. Garnish with cilantro and serve hot.

Vegetables, Avocado, White Bean Salad on toast:

Makes: 6 servings

Ingredients:

- 2 cans (16 ounce each) white beans (cannellini), drained, rinsed

- 2/3 cup onions, diced

- 1 cup spinach, thinly sliced

- 2 small avocadoes, peeled, pitted, diced

- 1 medium carrot, peeled, chopped

- 2 teaspoons apple cider vinegar

- Juice of 2 lemon

- 4 teaspoons miso paste

- 2 tablespoons sunflower seeds or hemp seeds

- 2 tablespoons orange juice

- 1/2 teaspoon orange zest, grated

- 4 tablespoons nutritional yeast

- 1/4 teaspoon cayenne pepper

- Salt to taste

- Pepper powder to taste

- 12 slice bread, toasted

- Fresh chives to serve

- 2 tablespoons fresh parsley

Instructions:

1. Place beans and avocadoes in a large bowl. Using a fork, mash it. Keep the consistency of mashing, as you desire.

2. Add spinach, carrots, and onions. Mix well.

3. Whisk together in a small bowl, miso paste, orange juice and vinegar. Add this to the salad bowl. Fold gently. Add nutritional yeast and mix well.

4. Place the salad over toasted bread. Garnish with chives and parsley and serve.

Vegan Frittata:

Makes: 8 servings

Ingredients:

- 3 1/2 cups cooked brown rice

- 2 egg replacer

- 1 red bell pepper, chopped

- 1 yellow bell pepper, chopped

- 8 spring onions, chopped (keep the white and green parts separately)

- 1 large onion, chopped

- 8 cloves garlic, peeled, crushed, chopped

- 1 cup kale, remove hard ribs and stem, chopped

- 1 cup baby spinach

- 1/2 cup fresh basil leaves

- 6 mushrooms, chopped

- 2 packages firm tofu

- 1 teaspoon ground turmeric

- 4 teaspoons Dijon mustard

- 4 tablespoons soy sauce or to taste

- 1 1/3 cups non dairy milk like soy milk or almond milk

- 2 tablespoons olive oil

- 4 teaspoons arrowroot

Instructions:

1. Mix together in a bowl, egg replacer and cooked brown rice. Transfer into 2 lightly greased spring form pans. Press the mixture well to the bottom of the pans.

2. Brush with a little oil all over the top of the mixture,

3. Bake in a preheated oven at 375 degree F for about 10 minutes.

4. Remove from the oven and keep aside.

5. Place a nonstick skillet over medium heat. Add oil. When oil is heated, add onions, garlic, and white parts of the green onions. Sauté until the onions are translucent.

6. Add bell peppers and mushrooms. Sauté for 7-8 minutes. Add spinach and kale. Mix well.

7. Add green parts of the green onions and basil. Mix well. Cook until the greens wilts.

8. Meanwhile, blend together in a food processor, tofu, mustard, soy sauce, turmeric, nutritional yeast, oil and arrowroot until smooth.

9. Transfer this mixture into the pan of greens. Mix well.

10. Now pour this mixture into the 2 baked pans. Spread it all over the pan.

11. Bake in a preheated oven at 350 degree F for about 35 - 40 minutes.

12. Remove from the oven and set aside to cool. When warm, slice into wedges and serve.

Southwestern Tofu n Beans Scramble Wrap:

Makes: 4 servings

Ingredients:

- 1 block (14 ounce) extra firm tofu
- 1 small onion, chopped
- 1 tablespoon grapeseed oil
- 1/2 a small red bell pepper, finely chopped
- 1/2 a small green bell pepper, finely chopped
- 1/2 a 15 ounce can black beans, rinsed, drained
- 1 teaspoon ground turmeric
- 1/4 teaspoon ground cumin
- 1/4 teaspoon ground coriander
- 2 tablespoons fresh cilantro, chopped
- Salt to taste
- Freshly ground pepper powder to taste
- 4 whole wheat tortillas
- 4 tablespoons salsa
- 1 avocado, peeled, pitted, chopped
- 2 scallions, sliced

- 4 tablespoons vegan cheddar cheese, grated

- A dash of hot sauce

Instructions:

1. Place the tofu on 3-4 layers of paper towels so as to drain any extra liquid. Mash the tofu using a potato masher or with your hands.

2. Place a skillet over medium high heat. Add grape seed oil. When oil is heated, add onions and bell peppers. Sauté until the onions are translucent.

3. Add ground coriander and cumin powder. Sauté until fragrant. Add turmeric and sauté for a few seconds.

4. Add tofu and beans. Stir well until thoroughly heated. Add cilantro, salt, and pepper. Mix well and remove from heat.

5. Warm the tortillas according to instructions on the package.

6. Divide the filling and place in the center of the tortillas. Sprinkle scallions, avocado, and cheese. Add a dash of hot sauce. Roll and serve.

Healthy Holiday Breakfast Pizza:

Makes: 8 servings

Ingredients:

- 2 sheets frozen puff pastry

- 2 containers (8 ounce each) vegan strawberry cream cheese

- 12 ounces fresh blackberries

- 12 ounces fresh raspberries

- 12 ounces fresh blueberries

- 16 ounces fresh strawberries

- 1/2 teaspoon almond extract

- 1 teaspoon vanilla bean paste

- 4 teaspoons sugar or sweetener of your choice

- A little powdered sugar to garnish (optional)

Instructions:

1. Thaw the puff pastry sheets according to the instructions given on the package. Cut the pastry sheets into 2 lengthwise to get 4 pieces in all.

2. Using a sharp knife, make diagonal cuts on the pastry sheet pieces to avoid puffing up when baking.

3. Place on a baking sheet and bake according to the instructions given on the package.

4. Remove from the oven and place on a wire rack. Let it cool completely.

5. Meanwhile, place 12 raspberries and 6 strawberries in a bowl and mash it with a fork. Add vegan cream cheese to it. Mix well. Add almond extract, vanilla paste and sugar to it. Mix well.

6. Spread this vegan cream cheese mixture on the baked puff pastry pieces.

7. Arrange the strawberries, blueberries, blackberries and raspberries in any manner you like.

8. Cut each piece into 2 pieces and serve.

Vegan Gingerbread Pancakes:

Makes: 6 servings of 4 pancakes in each serving

Ingredients:

For vegan egg:

- 2 tablespoons ground flaxseed

- 6 tablespoons water

For pancake:

- 2 cups whole wheat flour

- 2 teaspoons baking powder

- 2 scoops plant based vanilla protein powder

- 1 teaspoon ground ginger

- 2 teaspoons ground cinnamon

- 1/2 teaspoon freshly grated nutmeg

- 1/4 teaspoon ground cloves

- 2 teaspoons apple cider vinegar

- 2 tablespoons canola oil

- 3 cups vanilla soy milk

- 2 tablespoons pure maple syrup

- 1 teaspoon vanilla extract

- Cooking spray

Instructions:

1. To make vegan egg: Mix together flax meal and water in a small bowl and keep aside to thicken.

2. Meanwhile mix together in a large bowl, whole-wheat flour, baking powder, vanilla protein powder, ground ginger, cloves and cinnamon, and nutmeg.

3. To make vegan buttermilk: Mix together in another bowl, apple cider vinegar and soymilk. Add canola oil, vanilla extract and maple syrup. Mix well. Add vegan egg and mix well.

4. Add this mixture to the bowl of dry ingredients. Whisk until the entire contents are combined. Do not over mix.

5. Place a nonstick pan over medium heat. When the pan is hot (when you sprinkle a few drops of water, it should sizzle). Spray with cooking spray. Pour 2 tablespoons of batter on to the pan. Spread into small rounds of about 4 inches by swirling the pan. Slowly bubbles will start forming. Slightly lift the bottom side to check if it is cooked to medium brown color. If it is, then flip sides and cook the other side too.

6. If your pan is big enough, then make the pancakes in batches.

7. Repeat step 5 and 6 with the remaining batter.

8. Keep warm in the oven until use.

Fruit Parfait:

Makes: 4 servings

Ingredients:

For the red layer:

- 1 cup frozen strawberries
- 1 cup frozen raspberries
- 1/2 cup berry flavored soy yogurt
- 2 tablespoons maple syrup

For the green layer:

- 2 cups frozen kiwis
- 1 cup lemon flavored yogurt
- 2 tablespoons maple syrup

For the yellowish orange layer

- 1 cup frozen peach
- 1 cup frozen nectarine
- 1 cup mango flavored soy yogurt
- 2 tablespoons maple syrup
- 2 -3 tablespoons nuts of your choice

Instructions:

1. To make the red layer: Blend together strawberries, raspberries, maple syrup, and berry flavored yogurt until smooth. Pour into 4 tall glasses.

2. To make the green layer: Blend together, kiwis, maple syrup and lemon yogurt until smooth. Pour over the red layer.

3. To make the yellowish orange layer: Blend together peach, nectarine, mango yogurt and maple syrup. Pour over the green layer.

4. Chill in the freezer for about an hour. Garnish with almonds and serve.

Savory Oatmeal:

Makes: 4 servings

Ingredients:

- 2 cups old fashioned rolled oats
- 4 cups water
- Salt to taste
- 1 teaspoon curry powder
- 1/2 cup cashews, chopped, toasted
- 1/2 cup golden raisins

Instructions:

1. Pour water in a saucepan. Add salt and bring to a boil. Add oats and mix well.

2. Lower heat and cook until most of the water is absorbed.

3. Remove from heat. Cover the saucepan and let it sit for 2-3 minutes.

4. Add curry powder, cashews and raisins and mix well.

5. Serve in individual bowls.

Rice and Raisin Breakfast Pudding:

Makes: 4 servings

Ingredients:

- ½ cup water

- 1 ½ cups cooked brown rice

- ¼ cup raisins

- 2 tablespoons maple syrup

- ½ cup soy milk

- ¼ cup almonds, chopped, toasted

- ½ teaspoon ground cinnamon

- ¼ teaspoon ground cardamom

Instructions:

1. To a heavy bottomed saucepan add all the ingredients. Place the pot over medium heat. Bring to a boil.

2. Lower the heat and simmer for 6-8 minutes until it thickens. Stir in between a couple of times.

3. Serve in individual bowls.

Mexican Molletes with Mango Basil Salsa:

Makes: 4 servings

Ingredients:

- 4 bolillo rolls, split into 2 halves

For refried beans:

- 2 cups canned or cooked black beans (retain a little of the cooked water or liquid from the can)

- 1 medium onion, finely chopped

- 3 cloves garlic, crushed, minced

- 1 teaspoon olive oil

- 1 1/2 teaspoons cumin powder

- 1/4 teaspoon black pepper powder

- 1 chipotle chili pepper in abodo sauce, finely chopped

- Salt to taste

- 1/4 cup fresh cilantro, chopped

For mango salsa:

- 1 1/2 ripe mangoes, peeled, deseeded, chopped into small pieces

- 3 tablespoons red onion, finely chopped

- 8 basil leaves, chopped into thin strips

- 1 tablespoon lime juice

- 1 jalapeno pepper, minced

Instructions:

1. To make refried beans: Place a skillet over medium heat. Add oil. When oil is heated, add onions. Sauté for a few minutes until the onions are translucent. Add garlic, salt and pepper. Sauté until garlic is fragrant.

2. Add chipotle chili and cumin powder. Mix well and add cooked beans along with a cup of the cooked water. Bring to a boil.

3. Lower heat and let the contents simmer for a while. Add a little more water if the mixture becomes too dry. Remove from heat.

4. Mash the contents with a potato masher such that some of the bens remain whole and most of it is mashed.

5. Add cilantro and mix well

Breakfast Vegetable Miso Soup with Chickpeas:

Makes: 6 servings

Ingredients:

- 1 yellow onion, chopped

- 4 cloves garlic, minced

- 2 cups broccoli, chopped

- 2 cups cooked chickpeas

- 4 carrots, peeled, diced

- 4 celery stalks, diced

- 4 tablespoons white miso mixed with 1/4 cup of water

- Coarse salt to taste

- 4 tablespoons olive oil

- Pepper powder to taste

- 8 cups water

Instructions:

1. Place a pot over medium heat. Add oil. When oil is heated, add onions and garlic. Sauté until the onions are translucent. Add celery and carrots. Cook for 2-3 minutes.

2. Add broccoli and chickpeas. Mix well and stir-fry for a couple of minutes.

3. Add water and bring to boil. Lower heat and simmer until the vegetables are tender. Remove from heat.

4. Add miso, salt and pepper. Mix well and serve immediately.

Apple Spice Breakfast Soup:

Ingredients:

- 6 pink lady or any other tart apple, cored, diced

- 2 liters water

- 1 1/2 teaspoon ground nutmeg

- 1/2 teaspoon ground cloves

- 3/4 teaspoons ground allspice

- 1 cup raisins

- 3 tablespoons agave nectar

- 3/4 cup vanilla flavored coconut milk yogurt

- 3 tablespoons lemon juice

- 6 slices stale whole wheat bread, diced

Instructions:

1. Add water, apples, raisins, ground nutmeg, cinnamon, cloves and allspice, salt and agave to a large pot.

2. Place the pot over medium heat. Bring to a boil.

3. Lower heat and simmer for about an hour. Add diced bread. Mix well. Simmer for a couple of minutes.

4. Remove from heat. Add lemon juice and yogurt. Mix well and serve immediately. If you do not like it hot, then refrigerate until chilled and serve.

Tofu Spinach Quiche:

Makes: 4 servings

Ingredients:

- 2 containers (8 ounce each) tofu

- 2/3 cup almond milk or soy milk

- 1 teaspoon salt or to taste

- 1 teaspoon pepper or to taste

- 20 ounce frozen spinach, chopped, thawed, drained

- 2 teaspoon garlic, minced

- ½ cup onions, chopped

- 1 cup vegan cheese, cheddar flavored

- 1 cup vegan Swiss cheese

- 2 unbaked 9 inch pie crust

Instructions:

1. Blend together tofu and milk in a blender until smooth. If it is too thick, you can add more milk.

2. Transfer into a bowl. Season with salt and pepper. Add spinach, garlic, onions, cheeses and the blended tofu mixture. Stir well.

3. Divide the mixture amongst the 2 piecrusts.

4. Bake in a preheated oven for 30 minutes or until golden brown.

Veggies and Mushrooms Breakfast Bites:

Makes: 4 - 6 servings

Ingredients:

- 2 aubergines, chopped into bite sized pieces

- 2 small heads broccoli, chopped into bite sized pieces

- 1/2 head small cauliflower, chopped into bite sized pieces

- 4 carrots. Chopped into bite sized pieces

- 2 red peppers, chopped into bite sized pieces

- 2 green pepper, chopped into bite sized pieces

- 6 cloves garlic

- 1 cup baby spinach

- 1/2 cup cashews

- 1/2 cup olive oil

- 1 teaspoon ground ginger

- Salt to taste

To make marinated Portobello mushrooms:

- 2 cups Portobello mushrooms, halved or quartered according to the size

- Salt to taste

- 2 tablespoons olive oil

- 4 tablespoons balsamic vinegar

Instructions:

1. Add aubergines, carrots, broccoli, cauliflowers and peppers to a baking sheet. Sprinkle salt and drizzle some oil over it.

2. Bake in a preheated oven at 350 degree F for about 40 minutes. Remove from oven and let it cool for a while.

3. Peel the skin of the peppers and add to the food processer bowl to which the S blade has been fixed. Add rest of the baked vegetables and pulse for a few seconds.

4. Add spinach, cashews, garlic, and about 1/3 of the mushrooms, remaining oil, salt and ginger. Blend until smooth.

5. Remove from the blender. Using your hands make small bite sized balls of the mixture.

6. Serve as it is or bake for 10-15 minutes and then serve.

7. To make marinated Portobello mushrooms: Add all the ingredients of the marinated Portobello mushrooms to a jar. Close the lid of the jar. Refrigerate for at least a day.

8. Blend the marinated mushrooms along with the marinade until smooth. If it is too thick, add some water and blend again.

9. Serve with mushroom sauce. Garnish with nuts and sprouts.

Breakfast Oatmeal Risotto:

Makes: 6 servings

Ingredients:

- 2 cups steel cut oats
- 1 medium onion, minced
- 4 cloves garlic, minced
- 1/2 cup green bell pepper, minced
- 2 cups mushrooms, minced
- 1/4 cup sun dried tomatoes, minced
- 8-10 cups water or as per requirement
- 1 teaspoon dried marjoram
- 2 teaspoons dried oregano
- 2 teaspoons dried basil
- 1/4 teaspoon ground rosemary
- 4 tablespoons nutritional yeast
- Salt to taste
- Pepper powder to taste

Instructions:

1. Place a heavy bottomed pan over medium heat. Add oil. When oil is heated, add onions and sauté until it is pink. Add garlic, mushrooms, bell pepper, and all the dried herbs.

2. Sauté for a while until the mushrooms are brown. Add oats and stir constantly until it is lightly toasted.

3. Add sundried tomatoes and about 2 cups of water. Simmer the mixture and stir often.

4. Add another cup of water and continue simmering, stirring often.

5. Continue adding water until the oats are tender.

6. Add nutritional yeast, salt and pepper. Mix well and serve immediately.

Homemade Spicy Italian Vegan Sausage:

Makes: 8 sausages

Ingredients:

For Spice mix:

- 3 teaspoons garlic powder

- 3 teaspoons fennel, crushed

- 3 teaspoons sweet paprika

- 3 teaspoons smoked paprika

- 1 teaspoon black pepper powder

- 2 teaspoons salt

- 1 teaspoon red pepper flakes

- 2 teaspoons dried oregano

- 1/4 teaspoon allspice

For the sausage:

- 8 teaspoons olive oil, divided

- 1/2 cup onions, finely chopped

- 2 cups mushrooms

- 2 cloves garlic, minced

- 4 cups cooked black eyed peas (you can use canned ones too), rinsed, drained

- 1/2 cup nutritional yeast

- 2 tablespoons sun dried tomato paste

- 2 teaspoons xanthan gum

- 1 cup brown rice flour

- 6 tablespoons vegan Worcestershire sauce

- A few drops of liquid smoke (optional)

Instructions:

1. To make the spice mix: Mix together all the ingredients and keep it aside.

2. To make the sausages: Place a skillet over medium heat. Add half the olive oil. When oil is heated, add onions and garlic. Sauté until the onions are translucent. Add mushrooms. Sauté until the mushrooms are tender. Remove from heat and keep it aside to cool.

3. Add black-eyed peas to a large bowl. Mash with a potato masher or by using your hands. Add tomato paste, spice mix, nutritional yeast, and brown rice flour and mix it all well.

4. Sprinkle xanthan gum and mix until well combined. Mix the mushrooms to this. Add Worcestershire sauce and liquid smoke if you are using.

5. Mix well with your hands. Divide the mixture into 8 equal parts. Using your hands, shape into logs. Wrap each log in aluminum foil.

6. Steam the wrapped logs in a large pot of boiling water in batches.

7. Let it cool completely. Refrigerate for at least 7-8 hours. The longer you refrigerate, the firmer it gets.

8. To use: Remove the foil from the sausage. Cook as required in a grill pan and serve with any toppings you desire or sauté some onions and bell peppers.

Edamame Hummus:

Ingredients:

- 2 bags (6 cups) frozen shelled edamame

- 4 cloves garlic, peeled

- 1/2 cup tahini

- 1/2 cup water

- 1/2 cup fresh lemon juice

- 1 to 2 teaspoons fine grain sea salt or to taste

- 1/4 teaspoon cayenne pepper

- 1/2 teaspoon ground coriander

- Freshly ground black pepper to taste

- Smoked paprika to garnish

- Extra virgin olive oil to drizzle

Instructions:

1. Thaw the edamame. Rinse and drain.

2. Place a large saucepan of water over medium heat. Add edamame. Bring to a boil. Remove from heat, rinse and drain. If you have the patience, you can remove the skin of the edamame if you desire.

3. Add edamame to the food processor bowl. Add garlic and pulse until smooth.

4. Add lemon juice, tahini, and water and pulse until well combined. Add cayenne pepper and coriander.

5. Remove into a serving bowl. Sprinkle smoked paprika, freshly ground black pepper and drizzle some extra virgin olive oil over it.

6. Serve either with crostini or crackers or toasted pita chips etc.

Hummus:

Ingredients:

- 2 cans chickpeas (garbanzo beans), washed and drained

- 1 lemon, juiced

- 2 cloves garlic, minced

- ½ cup tahini or more to suit your taste

- 6 tablespoons olive oil

- 6 tablespoons water plus more if needed

- 1 teaspoon cumin

- Salt to taste

- Pepper powder, to taste

- Smoked paprika to taste (optional)

Instructions:

1. Blend together all the ingredients until smooth. Transfer into a serving bowl.

Thick Coconut Yogurt:

Makes: 4 servings

Ingredients:

- 4 cups fresh young Thai coconut meat

- 1 cup coconut water

- 2 tablespoons fresh lemon juice

- ½ to 1 teaspoon probiotic powder (optional)

- A pinch pink salt

- Liquid sweetener to taste

Instructions:

1. Add all the ingredients to a blender. Initially blend on low speed. Slowly increase the speed to high and blend until smooth.

2. Transfer the contents into an airtight container. Close the lid and refrigerate for a few hours.

3. Serve with a jam of your choice or granola.

4. 1234567890

Quinoa Porridge:

Makes: 4 servings

Ingredients:

- 1 cup quinoa
- ½ teaspoon ground cinnamon
- 3 cups almond milk
- 1 cup water
- ¼ cup brown sugar
- 1 teaspoon vanilla extract (optional)
- A large pinch salt

Instructions:

1. Place a thick-bottomed saucepan over medium heat. Add quinoa and roast for a couple of minutes until the quinoa is toasted. Add cinnamon and sauté for a few seconds.

2. Add almond milk, water, vanilla, salt, and brown sugar. Mix well.

3. Bring to a boil. Stir frequently.

4. Lower heat and simmer for about 30 minutes until the quinoa is cooked. If it is too, thick, add some more water or almond milk.

5. Serve hot or warm.

Breakfast Burrito Bake:

Makes: 4 to 6 servings

Ingredients:

- 3 medium russet potatoes, (peeled and shredded) steamed until soft

- 1 small yellow onion, finely chopped

- ½ red or orange bell pepper, chopped into small cubes

- 1 small zucchini, chopped into small cubes

- 4-5 white or cremini mushrooms, sliced

- ½ bunch greens (any of the following: kale, collards, chard, spinach, etc.) chopped into small pieces

- 1 ½ tablespoons nutritional yeast

- Juice from ½ a lime

- 1 tablespoon nutritional yeast

- 1 teaspoon dried basil

- ¾ teaspoon garlic powder

- 1 teaspoon oregano

- 1 teaspoon chili powder

- ¼ teaspoon red pepper flakes

- ½ a 15 ounce can diced tomatoes

- ½ a 15 ounce can black beans

- ½ a 15 ounce can pinto beans

- ¼ cup chopped fresh cilantro leaves

- Cooking spray

- Water as required

- Pumpkin seeds, toasted for garnishing (optional)

Instructions:

1. Divide the steamed potatoes into 2 bowls.

2. In one of the bowls add 1-tablespoon nutritional yeast and mix well. Keep aside.

3. Place a skillet over medium heat. Spray with cooking spray.

4. Add onions, bell pepper, zucchini, and mushrooms and sauté for a few minutes. Add water if needed (if it is getting stuck).

5. Add lime juice, oregano, garlic powder, red pepper flakes, and basil. Mix well. Add ½ tablespoon nutritional yeast and the bowl of potatoes that does not contain nutritional yeast.

6. Remove from heat and add tomatoes, cilantro, black beans and pinto beans. Transfer into an ovenproof glass-baking dish. Spread it evenly to cover the dish.

7. Spread with potato mixture (the bowl that contained nutritional yeast) to cover as much area as possible.

8. Bake in a preheated oven at 375 degree F for about 45 minutes or until the top is light to golden brown, depending on your choice.

9. Cool for 5-7 minutes and serve with toasted pumpkin seeds.

Blushing Apple Smoothie

Ingredients:

- 1 apple (medium to large sized)

- ½ cup cherries

- ½ English cucumber

- ½ cup raspberries

- 1 tablespoon chia seeds

- Around 7 or 8 ice cubes

- ½ cup water

Instructions:

1. Before you begin, make sure that the raspberries and cherries are quite fresh. If not the smoothie may end up tasting a little brackish.

2. The cherries should be pitted and the cucumber cut into small chunks.

3. Once you are done with all these preliminary preparations, add all the ingredients into the blender and process for at least 30 seconds. You can of course go for a longer duration if you desire a more soft and creamy consistency to your smoothie.

Sleepy Blueberry Muffin Smoothie

Ingredients:

- ½ cup blueberries

- 1 teaspoon vanilla extract

- 1 tablespoon chia seeds

- 11/2 cup of non-diary milk such as almond milk or soy milk

- 1 tablespoon protein powder (vanilla)

- 2 tablespoons oats

Instructions:

1. Like many other smoothies, the ingredients to this one should also be prepared a few hours in advance (a minimum of 4 hours is recommended). But as I have mentioned earlier, you end up getting the best results if the preliminary steps are done the night before.

2. Another fact to be noted here is that you have other options as well when it comes to the choice of oats. You can go for regular oats or the gluten free versions of it. Alternatively quinoa and quinoa flakes can also be used.

3. Take a medium sized plastic or glass bowl and mix together all the ingredients except the blueberries, which should be added only a second before blending.

4. Store the bowl in a refrigerator overnight.

5. In the morning, empty the bowl into the blender, add the blueberries and process for half a minute.

Raspberry Poppy Seed Lemon Smoothie

Ingredients:

- ½ cup raspberries

- 11/2 teaspoon poppy seeds

- 1 tablespoon lemon juice

- 1 ½ cups non-diary milk

- 2 tablespoon oats

- 1 tablespoon chia seeds

- Zest of a small lemon

- A pinch of stevia powder (white)

- 1 tablespoon almond butter

- A little extra lemon and raspberries as topping

Instructions:

1. The ingredients to this smoothie should be prepared a few hours in advance (a minimum of 4 hours is recommended). But as is my experience, you end up getting the best results if the preliminary steps are done the night before.

2. Take a medium sized plastic or glass bowl and mix together all the ingredients. Now give a few good shakes. For this purpose, Mason jars are the best

option. Now let the jar be refrigerated till you use it in the morning.

3. In the morning, empty the jar into the blender and process for a good 40 seconds.

High Energy Smoothies

This smoothie can be made in two distinct flavors; strawberry banana flavor and blueberry peach flavor. I have mentioned all the ingredients below, but you can decide to omit the strawberries and bananas or inversely the blueberries and peaches based on your preference.

Ingredients:

- Half a banana

- 5 or 6 strawberries

- 1 cup of blueberries

- Half a peach

- 1 helping of probiotics

- 1 scoop of protein powder

- 1 cup green tea

- 1 tablespoon chia seeds

Instructions:

1. The ingredients to this smoothie should be prepared at least 4 hours in advance. But it is recommended that you keep the mixed ingredients overnight for the best results.

2. Take a medium sized plastic or glass bowl and mix together all the ingredients. Now give a few good shakes. For this purpose, Mason jars are the best

option. Now let the jar be refrigerated till you use it in the morning.

3. Empty the jar into the blender in the morning and process for a good 40 seconds.

4. You can run the blender for a longer time if you like your smoothies to be as soft as cream.

Sleepy Banana Muffin Smoothie

Ingredients:

- 1 medium to large banana

- 2 tablespoons walnuts

- 1 tablespoon raisins

- A pinch of cinnamon (ground)

- 11/4 cup of non-dairy milk (you can opt for either almond milk or soy milk)

- 1 tablespoon oats (regular)

- ½ tablespoon vanilla extract

- Optional toppings (These can anything from shredded coconut shavings or raisins, walnuts or chocolate chips or anything else that catches your imagination)

Instructions:

1. The ingredients to this smoothie should be prepared at least 4 hours in advance. But it is recommended that you keep the mixed ingredients overnight for the best results.

2. Take a medium sized plastic or glass bowl and mix together all the ingredients. Note that you do not have the entire amount of milk at this stage; 1 cup will do.

3. Now give a few good shakes. For this purpose, Mason jars are the best option. Now let the jar be refrigerated till you use it in the morning.

4. Empty the jar into the blender in the morning and process for a good half a minute, after adding the rest of the milk.

5. Finish off the smoothie by using the toppings.

Spicy Pumpkin Smoothie

Ingredients:

- ½ cup canned pumpkin (you can use canned pumpkins as well)

- 1 cup of non-diary milk (almond or soy milk)

- 1-tablespoon raisins. You can alternatively make use of half a teaspoon of maple syrup

- ½ banana (medium sized)

- Some vegan whipped coconut cream

- 1/8 teaspoon ground ginger

- ¼ teaspoon cinnamon (ground)

- ½ teaspoon vanilla extract

- A pinch of all spice

- A pinch of nutmeg (ground)

- A pinch of cloves

Instructions:

1. Take all the ingredients except the coconut cream and mix it together in a bowl.

2. Let it stand for 15 minutes and transfer the contents into a blender.

3. Process the contents of the blender for a good 40 seconds.

4. You can run the blender for a longer time if you like your smoothies to be on the extra soft side.

5. Once the blending is done, pour the contents into a glass and top it off with a few scoops of the coconut cream. Sprinkle a little cinnamon on top of the glass.

Chocolate chip Cookie Dough Smoothie

Ingredients:

- 1 tablespoon cacao powder

- 11/4 cup of non-diary milk. (You can stick with the unsweetened version if you don't want your smoothie to be too sweet.)

- 1 tablespoon of almond butter

- ¼ teaspoon of vanilla extract

- 6 tablespoons of oats (you can use quinoa as well)

- 1 tablespoon chia seeds

Instructions:

1. The ingredients to this smoothie should be prepared at least 4 hours in advance. But it is recommended that you keep the mixed ingredients overnight for the best results.

2. Take a medium sized plastic or glass bowl and mix together all the ingredients. Note that you do not have the entire amount of milk at this stage; 1 cup will do.

3. Now give a few good shakes. For this purpose, Mason jars are the best option. Now let the jar be refrigerated till you use it in the morning.

4. Empty the jar into the blender in the morning and process for a good half a minute, after adding the rest of the milk.

5. Use any leftover cacao powder as topping.

Classic Greens Smoothie

Ingredients:

- 2 cups of organic spinach

- 1 cup of non-diary milk. As in the case of most vegan dishes, you can make use of either almond milk or soymilk.

- 1 banana (medium sized and frozen)

- 1 tablespoon of almond butter (raw is preferred)

- 2 tablespoon flax seeds (ground)

- 3 or 4 ice cubes.

Instructions:

1. This is one composite and flexible smoothie. That means that you can pretty much throw in any green vegetable that you prefer.

2. Take a medium sized plastic or glass bowl and mix together all the ingredients. Now give a few good shakes.

3. Empty the jar into the blender and process for a good 30 seconds.

Apple Caramel Smoothie

Ingredients:

- 1 medium sized apple (sliced and frozen)

- 1 cup of non-diary milk. You can make use of either almond milk or soymilk.

- 2 dates (pitted medjool)

- 2 cups of spinach

- 1/8 teaspoon cinnamon (ground)

- 2 tablespoons sun butter

- ¼ teaspoon vanilla extract

- 2 or 3 ice cubes

- A pinch of salt

Instructions:

1. Take a medium sized plastic or glass bowl and mix together all the ingredients. Now give a few good shakes so that everything gets mixed well.

2. Empty the jar into the blender and process for a good 30 seconds. Blend more if you want a more fine texture to the smoothie.

Lime Green Smoothie

Ingredients:

- 2 tablespoons of lime juice

- 1 medium sized banana (ripe and frozen)

- 1 teaspoon lime zest

- 1 cup non-diary milk (almond or soy milk)

- ¼ spoon vanilla extract

- 1 medjool date (pitted)

- 2 cups of baby spinach (organic)

- 1 tablespoon sunflower butter

- 4 or 5 ice cubes

- A few crackers to taste

Instructions:

1. Take a medium sized plastic or glass bowl and mix together all the ingredients. Now give a few good shakes so that everything gets mixed well.

2. Empty the jar into the blender and process for a good 30 seconds. Blend more if you want a more fine texture to the smoothie.

Ultra Green Avocado Smoothie

Ingredients:

- ½ banana (medium sized and frozen)

- ½ avocado (frozen)

- 1 cup of non-diary milk. You can use either almond milk or soymilk, but the unsweetened version is preferred.

- 2 cups of spinach (organic)

- 2-tablespoon hemp hearts. You can use hemp seeds as well.

- A few ice cubes

Instructions:

1. Take a medium sized plastic or glass bowl and mix together all the ingredients. Now give a few good shakes so that everything gets mixed well.

2. Empty the jar into the blender and process for a good 30 seconds. Blend more if you want a more fine texture to the smoothie.

The Superman Smoothie

As the name suggests, this is one real power smoothie packed with nutrients! So let us see how it is made.

Ingredients:

- 1 cup spinach

- 1 tablespoon almond butter

- 1 cup non-diary milk (almond milk or soy milk)

- 1 tablespoon cacao powder

- 1 tablespoon coconut oil

- 1 teaspoon spirulina

- 1 tablespoon honey

- 1 cup frozen berries

- 5 or 6 ice cubes

Instructions:

1. Take a medium sized plastic or glass bowl and mix together all the ingredients. Now give a few good shakes so that everything gets mixed well.

2. Empty the jar into the blender and process for a good 30 seconds. Blend more if you want a more fine texture to the smoothie.

Raspberry Chocolate Smoothie

Ingredients:

- 1 cup raspberries

- 2 tablespoons of shredded coconut

- 2 cups organic spinach

- 1 cup of non-diary milk (almond milk or soy milk)

- 2 tablespoon flax seeds (ground)

- 1 tablespoon cacao powder

- 2 or 3 ice cubes

Instructions:

1. Take a medium sized plastic or glass bowl and mix together all the ingredients. Now give a few good shakes so that everything gets mixed well.

2. Empty the jar into the blender and process for a good 30 seconds. Blend more if you want a more fine texture to the smoothie.

Cinnamon Walnut Waffles

Ingredients:

- 1 cup chopped walnuts

- 1 teaspoon cinnamon (ground)

- 2 cups of almond milk

- 2 cups of wheat flour

- 1 tablespoon baking powder

- 3 tablespoons olive oil

- ½ cup of water

- 3 tablespoons maple syrup

- 2 tablespoons flax seeds (ground)

- 1 teaspoon vanilla extract

- 1 cup dried figs (black)

- 1 tablespoon apple cider vinegar

- ½ teaspoon salt

Instructions:

1. Let us begin by curdling the apple cider vinegar and the almond milk. Add both of them into a bowl and set it aside.

2. In another bowl, mix together the flour, baking powder, salt and cinnamon.

3. Now add the flax seeds to the milk bowl that we had set aside earlier and beat it till the mixture turns frothy. Add this to the flour bowl along with the olive oil, maple syrup, vanilla and water.

4. Keep stirring with a wooden spoon or ladle, simultaneously adding the walnuts and the dried figs.

5. Now it is time to heat up the waffle iron. Once hot, brush the iron with cooking oil and pour in the waffle batter. Once the waffles are made, you can use any leftover walnuts or figs for garnishing.

Pancake

Ingredients:

- 1 tablespoon vegetable oil

- 1 green onion, finely chopped

- 1/4 cup finely chopped red bell pepper

- 1/2 cup chickpea flour

- 1/4 teaspoon garlic powder, or crushed garlic cloves

- 1/4 teaspoon fine grain sea salt

- 1/8 teaspoon freshly ground black pepper

- 1/4 teaspoon baking powder

- A pinch of red pepper flakes

- 1/2 cup ? (veg oil ?)

- Any sauce of your choice, to serve

Instructions:

1. Add the oil to a pan and allow it to heat.

2. Toss in the green onions and sauté until golden.

3. Add in the bell peppers, garlic powder and allow these to soften.

4. Meanwhile, add the chickpea flour to a bowl along with the salt and pepper.

5. Add baking powder, red pepper flakes and ½ cup water and give it a mix.

6. Add in the onion mix to the batter.

7. Heat a flat pan or griddle.

8. You can add a little vegetable oil if you like, use a ladle to scoop up the batter and pour over the griddle.

9. Allow it to bubble and firm up on one side before turning it to the other side.

10. Once it is done, place it on a plate and serve hot with any sauce of your choice.

Mixed vegetables

Ingredients:

- 2 cups diced sweet potatoes

- 2 teaspoons olive oil

- 1/2 cup diced red onion

- 2 cloves garlic, minced

- 1 cup mixed vegetables, sliced (peas, squash, potatoes, beans etc.)

- 2 tablespoons paprika

- 1/4 teaspoon cayenne pepper

- 3 cups Brussels sprouts, quartered

- 1 medium red pepper, diced

- 2 tablespoons lemon juice

- Chopped parsley, to garnish

- Salt to taste

- Pepper to taste

Instructions:

1. Place some water on the boil and add in the sweet potatoes and the mixed vegetables.

2. Allow them to soften up.

3. Meanwhile, add the olive oil to a pan along with the red onions and allow them to turn golden brown.

4. Add in the garlic and further sauté the mixture.

5. Add in the sprouts, red pepper, paprika, and cayenne and give it a good mix.

6. Toss in the pre-cooked sweet potatoes and veggies and give it all a good mix.

7. Add in the salt and pepper along with the limejuice and mix well.

8. Place the veggies on a plate and garnish with fresh parsley leaves.

9. Serve hot.

Blueberry delight

Ingredients:

- 1 cup whole wheat flour

- 1 tablespoon baking powder

- 1/2 teaspoon salt

- 1/4 teaspoon ground allspice

- 1 cup cooking oats

- 1/3 cup semi sweet applesauce

- 1 1/2 cups unsweetened almond milk (or any vegan milk)

- 3 tablespoons pure maple syrup

- 2 tablespoons canola oil

- 1 teaspoon pure vanilla extract

- 2 cups frozen blueberries

Instructions:

1. Start by adding the flour and baking soda along with the salt to a fine sieve.

2. Sieve it together twice or thrice to remove any impurities and to mix them all together.

3. Add to a bowl along with the all spice and give it a good mix.

4. Add in the applesauce and almond milk and give it a good mix.

5. Add in the vanilla extract and mix until well combined.

6. Heat a pan and add in the canola oil.

7. Use a ladle to spoon the batter on the pan and make tiny pancakes.

8. In a small bowl, add the maple syrup along with the blueberries and mix until well combined.

9. Spoon this mix over the pancakes and serve hot.

10. You can also spoon the maple syrup separately or replace it with honey.

Banana Pancake

Ingredients:

- 2 cups whole wheat flour

- 2 teaspoons baking powder

- ½ teaspoon sea salt

- 2 eggs, beaten

- 2 bananas, mashed (ideally 1 cup)

- 2 cups unsweetened, unflavored almond or any vegan milk

- 1 cup water

- 1 cup fresh or frozen strawberries, to garnish

- 1 sprig mint leaves, to garnish

- 1 teaspoon almond butter

Instructions

1. Start by adding the wheat flour, baking powder and salt to a sieve and sieve at least twice to mix them well.

2. Add in the beaten eggs along with the bananas and give it all a good mix.

3. Add in the vegan milk and mix until well combined.

4. The mixture should not be too thick or too thin.

5. Add in the water and give it a good mix.

6. Heat a pan or griddle and add in ½ teaspoon butter.

7. Spoon the pancake batter over it and allow the batter to bubble up on all sides.

8. Place the pancakes on a plate and garnish with cut strawberries and mint leaves.

9. Serve hot.

Spinach Quiche

For the crust

- 3 medium-large potatoes (around 3 cups)

- 2 tablespoons melted vegan butter

- 1/4 teaspoon sea salt

- ¼ teaspoon pepper

For the filling

- 12 ounces extra firm silken tofu, patted dry

- 2 tablespoon yeast

- 3 tablespoon humus

- Sea salt and black pepper, to taste

- 3 garlic cloves, chopped

- 2 red onions, thinly sliced

- 3/4 cup cherry tomatoes, halved

- 1 cup chopped broccoli

Instructions:

1. Preheat the oven to 450 degrees Fahrenheit.

2. Grate the potatoes and add to a bowl.

3. Add in the melted butter, salt and pepper and mix until well combined.

4. Line the base of a pie dish and stick it into the oven for 20 to 25 minutes or until golden.

5. On another tray, add in the vegetables along with the garlic and drizzle some oil on top.

6. Bake in the oven until well roasted.

7. Meanwhile, add the tofu to a blender along with the yeast, hummus, salt and pepper and blend it well together.

8. Add in the vegetables to the batter and give it a good mix.

9. Remove the crust from the oven and ladle the filling inside.

10. Place in the oven and bake for 30 minutes.

11. Serve the quiche hot.

Easy, healthy Soup

Ingredients:

- 2 pounds broccoli with stems

- ½ medium red onion, roughly chopped

- 1 small potato, scrubbed and roughly chopped

- 1 teaspoon garlic powder

- 2 cups green peas (fresh or frozen)

- Freshly ground black pepper (as per taste)

- 3 tablespoons lemon juice

- 1 tablespoon fresh dill (finely chopped)

- Sea salt to taste

- Pepper powder to taste

Instructions:

1. Place some water on the boil.

2. Add in the broccoli, red onion and potato and allow it to soften.

3. Add in the peas and garlic powder to a blender and puree it.

4. Add it to a saucepan and allow it to boil.

5. Once the vegetables soften, add it to a blender and puree it.

6. Add the puree to the green pea's mixture and mix until well combined.

7. Add in the pepper, salt, lemon juice and mix well.

8. Serve the soup in a bowl and top with the chopped dill.

9. Serve hot.

10. You can add a teaspoon of fresh vegan cream on top before serving.

Mixed lentils

Ingredients:

- 2 tablespoons olive oil

- 1 medium white onion, finely chopped

- 1 clove garlic, thinly sliced

- 1 tablespoon tomato paste

- 1 cup green lentils

- 1 cup red beans, soaked

- 2 tablespoons low sodium soya sauce

- Sea salt to taste

- Freshly ground black pepper to taste

- Parsley leaves, to garnish

Instructions:

1. Place some water on the boil.

2. Add in the lentils and beans and cook until soft.

3. Add the oil to a pan and heat it.

4. Add in the finely sliced onions and give it a good mix.

5. Add in the garlic cloves and sauté it until golden.

6. Add the tomato paste to it along with the soy sauce and a little water to make a curry out of it.

7. Add the soya sauce, sea salt and pepper and give it a good mix.

8. You can replace the pepper with red paprika if you like.

9. Add in the precooked lentils and beans and give it a good mix.

10. Place in a serving bowl and top with the parsley and serve hot.

Easy Flat Bread With Avocado Filling

Ingredients:

- 2 cups wheat flour

- 1/2 teaspoon fine grain sea salt

- 1/2 teaspoon baking soda

- 3/4 cup almost boiling water

- 1 tablespoon extra-virgin olive oil

- 1 avocado

- 1 small red onion, finely chopped

- ½ garlic clove, chopped

- 1 teaspoon Lime juice

- ¼ green Chili

- Salt to taste

- Paprika to taste

- Cherry tomatoes

- Cucumber slices

Instructions:

1. Add the wheat flour to a bowl along with the salt, soda and water and knead it into firm dough.

2. Set it aside for 10 minutes, you can add in a little water to it if you don't want it to stick.

3. Meanwhile, cut the avocado and scoop out the flesh.

4. Add it to a bowl along with the garlic and give it a good mix.

5. Add in the salt and limejuice along with the chili and mix well.

6. Add the tomato and cucumber to a bowl along with the paprika and salt and give it a good mix.

7. Place a pan on the heat and add in a little oil.

8. Make tiny balls out of the dough and roll them out into circles using a rolling pin.

9. Sprinkle some flour over them to prevent sticking.

10. Place the roundlets on the pan and allow to brown on both sides.

11. Place on a plate, top with the avocado and cherry tomatoes and serve hot.

Pistachio bread

Ingredients:

- 1 cup shelled pistachios, toasted and chopped coarsely

- 2 cups all-purpose flour

- 1/2 teaspoons baking soda

- 2 teaspoons baking powder

- 1/2 teaspoons salt

- 2/3 cups sugar

- 1 cup coconut milk

- 1/2 cup vegetable oil

- 2 teaspoons vanilla

- Fresh pistachios to garnish

Instructions:

1. Preheat the oven to 450 degrees Fahrenheit.

2. Add the flour, baking soda and baking powder along with the salt to a sieve and sieve it twice.

3. Add it to a bowl and set aside

4. In another bowl add the sugar and oil and cream it together until it turns fluffy.

5. Add in the along coconut milk and vanilla and give everything a good mix.

6. Add in the dry flour to the wet mix and mix until well combined.

7. Add in the pistachios and mix it well.

8. Place the better in a greased bread tin and stick it into the oven.

9. Bake for 35 to 40 minutes or until the bread evenly rises and develops a crack in the center.

10. Serve cut slices along with cut pistachios and serve.

Scrambled Kale

Ingredients:

- 1 red bell pepper, diced
- 8 ounces mushrooms, sliced
- 2 cloves garlic, minced
- 14 ounces tofu, firm, crumbled
- 1 1/2 teaspoons smoked paprika
- 1 teaspoon ground cumin
- 1 teaspoon salt to taste)
- 1/4 teaspoon turmeric
- 1 bunch kale, stems and leaves thinly sliced
- Some more salt & pepper, to taste

Instructions:

1. Place a pan on heat.
2. Add in the pepper, mushrooms and garlic and cook until soft.
3. Add in the crumbled tofu to it along with the cumin, salt and turmeric and mix everything together until well combined.
4. Add in the kale and stir it until well combined.

5. Cover it and cook for some time.

6. Serve hot and sprinkle additional salt and pepper before serving.

Chocolate Oat Treat

Ingredients:

- 2 cups plain almond milk

- 2 fully-ripened large bananas

- 1/4 teaspoon almond extract

- 1/4 teaspoon vanilla extract

- ½ teaspoon salt

- 2 cups rolled oats

- 2 tablespoons unsweetened cocoa powder

- 2 tablespoons honey

- 1/3 cup toasted and chopped walnuts

- ½ teaspoon ground cinnamon

- 2 tablespoons semisweet chocolate chips

Instructions:

1. Add the almond milk, water, and bananas, vanilla and salt to a pan and bring to a boil.

2. Add in the cinnamon powder, oats, coco powder and honey and allow it to cook.

3. You can cover it if you like.

4. Meanwhile, chop up the bananas and add it to 2-3 bowls.

5. Add in the honey, chocolate chips and give it a mix.

6. Add in the oat mix and serve hot.

Indian Crepes

Ingredients:

- 1 cup parboiled rice
- 1 cup white rice
- ¼ cup flattened rice
- ½ cup spilt black lentils
- ¼ teaspoon fenugreek seeds
- Oil
- 1 teaspoon Salt
- Water for grinding (about 2 cups)
- 1 cup boiled potatoes
- ½ green chilies
- Salt to taste

Instructions:

- Add the rice, par boiled rice and black lentils to enough water and soak for a few hours.
- At night, add it to a mixer along with the flattened rice and fenugreek seeds and blend it until well combined.
- Remove it into a bowl and add in the salt and water and make a thin batter out of it.

- You can then mix it with your hand to help it ferment overnight.

- Next morning, heat the pan and add oil to it.

- Use a ladle to place the batter and spread it around using the back of the ladle.

- Allow it to crisp up.

- In a small pan, add in a little oil along with the potatoes, chilies and salt and give it a good mix.

- Place the potato mix inside the crepes and serve hot.

Chapter 4:
High Protein Vegan Breakfast Recipes

Vegan Migas

Protein per serving: 14 g

Makes: 6 servings

Ingredients:

For Salsa Ranchera:

- 9 large ripe tomatoes

- 4 jalapeno or Serrano chilies

- 4 cloves garlic, unpeeled

- 3 tablespoons canola oil

- 3/4 teaspoon salt

For Vegan Migas:

- 21 ounce soft tofu, drained, place in a strainer to remove any excess moisture, crumbled

- 5 stale corn tortillas, torn into strips

- 2 tablespoons canola oil, divided

- 1/4 teaspoon ground turmeric

- 6 scallions, trimmed, chopped

- 3 jalapeno or Serrano chilies, finely chopped (deseed if you do not like it spicy)

- 3/4 teaspoon ground chipotle chili

- Salt to taste

- 3/4 cup non-dairy cheese, shredded

- 12 corn tortillas, warmed according to the instructions on the package

- 3 plum tomatoes, diced

- 1/3 cup fresh cilantro, chopped

Instructions:

1. To make Salsa Ranchera: Place a cast iron skillet over medium heat. Add tomatoes, garlic and chilies. Cook until the skin of the tomatoes is charred. Turn the tomatoes, garlic and chilies in between a few times. Remove them one by one as they get charred.

2. Peel the garlic when cool enough to handle and blend the ingredients in a blender until smooth.

3. Place the skillet back on heat. Add oil. When oil is heated, add the blended mixture. Add salt and mix well. Cook until the mixture is thick.

4. Remove from heat and transfer into a bowl. Cover and set aside.

5. To make Vegan Migas: Place a nonstick skillet over medium heat. Add 1/2-tablespoon oil. Add tortillas to it and cook until crisp and golden in color. Remove from the skillet and set aside on a plate.

6. Place the pan back on heat. Add the remaining oil. When oil is heated, add tofu and sauté for a couple of minutes.

7. Add turmeric, chilies, chipotle chili powder, scallions and salt. Stir often and cook until the moisture almost dries up.

8. Add cilantro, tomatoes, cheese, and the cooked, crisp tortillas strips. Sauté for a couple of minutes until the cheese melts.

9. To serve: Place 2 tortillas in each plate. Divide the tofu mixture between the 6 plates. Serve about 1/4 cup of Salsa Ranchera in each of the plates.

Breakfast Burrito:

Protein per serving: 15 g

Makes: 4 servings

Ingredients:

- 4 whole wheat tortillas (8 inches each)

- 2 cups extra firm tofu, crumbled

- Salt to taste

- Pepper powder to taste

- 1/2 cup fresh salsa

- 1/2 cup vegan Monterey Jack cheese, grated

- 1 tablespoon olive oil

Instructions:

1. Place a nonstick skillet over medium heat. Add oil. When oil is heated, add tofu. Sauté until it is light brown.

2. Add salsa, salt and pepper.

3. Sprinkle cheese on the center of the tortillas. Place tofu mixture over it. Roll and serve.

Jack O Pumpkin Breakfast Sandwich:

Protein per serving: 18 g

Makes: 4 servings

Ingredients:

For pumpkin butter:

- 2 cups canned pumpkin puree

- 1/4 teaspoon pumpkin pie spice

- 4 tablespoons maple syrup

- 3 tablespoons olive oil

- Salt to taste

For sandwich:

- 4 vegan sausage patties

- 4 whole wheat English muffins toasted

- 2 cups mushrooms, sliced

- 2 teaspoons olive oil

- Freshly ground black pepper powder to taste

- 2 cups arugula, chopped

- 4 teaspoons hot sauce (optional)

- 4 thick slices vegan Monterey Jack cheese

Instructions:

1. To make pumpkin butter: Add all the ingredients of the pumpkin butter into a microwave safe bowl. Whisk well.

2. Microwave on high for 30 seconds. Mix well and set-aside until use.

3. Apply olive oil with a brush over the vegan sausage patties and mushrooms. Sprinkle pepper powder over it.

4. Place a nonstick pan over medium high heat. Add patties and cook until brown on both the sides. Remove the patties and place it on a plate. Add mushrooms to the same pan. Cook for a few minutes until brown. Remove from pan and keep aside.

5. Place some mushrooms on each of the patty. Place a slice of cheese over the mushrooms. Place the entire patty (with mushrooms and cheese) back to the pan. Cover and cook for a couple of minutes until the cheese melts.

6. Spread 2 tablespoons pumpkin butter over the muffins on both the sides. Place the patty over it. Place arugula over the patty and a dash of hot sauce.

7. Serve warm immediately.

Sweet Potato and Brussels sprouts Hash:

Protein per serving: 24 grams

Makes: 6 servings

Ingredients:

- 3 cups sweet potatoes, diced
- 3/4 cup onions, diced
- 3 cloves garlic, minced
- 3 teaspoons olive oil
- 18 ounces veggie crumbles
- 5 cups Brussels sprouts, quartered
- 1 large red bell pepper, diced
- 3 tablespoons paprika
- 1/2 teaspoon cayenne pepper
- 1/3 cup parsley, chopped
- 3 tablespoons lemon juice
- Salt to taste
- Pepper powder to taste

Instructions:

1. Place a pot of water (about 8-10 cups of water) over medium heat. Add sweet potatoes. Bring to a boil and simmer until the sweet potatoes are soft.

2. Drain the excess water and keep it aside.

3. Place a large skillet over medium high heat. Add oil. When oil is hot, add onions and garlic. Sauté until the onions are translucent.

4. Add veggie crumbles paprika and cayenne pepper. Sauté for a couple of minutes.

5. Add Brussels sprouts and cook for about 5 minutes. Stir a couple of times in between.

6. Add red bell pepper and sweet potatoes. Cook for 3-4 minutes.

7. Add lemon juice, parsley, salt and pepper.

8. Mix well and serve hot.

Avocado Veggie Panini:

Protein per serving: 15 grams

Makes: 6 servings

Ingredients:

- 3 teaspoons butter
- 1 1/2 cups baby Portobello mushrooms, sliced
- 2 shallots, minced
- 1 1/2 cups cherry tomatoes, halved
- 3 medium avocadoes, peeled, pitted, mashed
- 3 cups kale, hard stems and ribs removed, chopped
- 12 thick slices whole wheat bread
- 6 slices vegan mozzarella cheese
- Salt to taste

Instructions:

1. Place a skillet over medium high heat. Add butter. When butter melts, add shallots. Sauté until the shallots are translucent.

2. Add mushrooms and sauté until the mushrooms are light brown.

3. Add tomatoes and kale. Sauté until the kale wilts and the tomatoes are thoroughly heated.

4. Remove from heat. Sprinkle salt and mix well.

5. Spread a layer of avocado on each of the bread slices.

6. Place the cooked vegetables on 6 of the bread slices. Place cheese slices over it. Cover with the remaining bread slices.

7. Place the prepared sandwiches in a preheated Panini press and cook until the bread is brown from outside.

Peanutty Quinoa Bowls with Baked Tofu:

Peanutty quinoa bowl:

Protein per serving: 15.6 grams

Baked Tofu:

Protein per serving: 11 grams

Makes: 4 servings

Ingredients:

For peanutty quinoa bowls:

- 1 cup quinoa

- 2 teaspoons olive oil

- 2 small broccoli heads, broken into florets

- 1 large red bell pepper, seeded, diced

- 2 teaspoons tamari or soy sauce

- 4 tablespoons peanut butter

- 4 tablespoons water

- 2 tablespoons fresh lime juice

- 1 teaspoon brown sugar

- Salt to taste

- Pepper powder to taste

- 4 tablespoons roasted peanuts, chopped

- 1 teaspoon fresh ginger, grated

For the baked tofu:

- 1 1/2 package (15 ounce each) extra firm tofu, cut into 8 thick slices

- 4 tablespoons tamari or soy sauce

- 1 1/2 tablespoons maple syrup

- 1 1/2 tablespoons olive oil

- 2 cloves garlic, minced

- Freshly ground black pepper powder to taste

- Cooking spray

Instructions:

1. To make peanutty quinoa bowls: Cook the quinoa according to the instructions given on the package.

2. Meanwhile, place a skillet over medium high heat. Add olive oil. When oil is hot, add red bell pepper. Sauté for a couple of minutes until it is soft. Remove and place in a large bowl.

3. To the same pan add broccoli. Also add 2 to 3 tablespoons of water. Cook the broccoli until it is tender. Transfer into the bowl in which red pepper is placed.

4. Whisk together peanut butter, lime juice, 4 tablespoons water, soy sauce, ginger and sugar until smooth.

5. Transfer the cooked quinoa into the bowl of vegetables. Pour the peanut sauce. Add salt and pepper. Mix well.

6. Divide the peanutty quinoa into 4 individual serving bowls. Sprinkle roasted peanuts over it.

7. Meanwhile, as the quinoa is cooking, prepare the baked tofu as follows: Add soy sauce, maple syrup, olive oil, garlic, and black pepper powder to a small baking dish. Whisk well.

8. Place the tofu slices in the baking dish. Coat the tofu well with the marinade. Keep aside for at least 30 minutes to an hour. Flip sides of the tofu on and off. The longer you marinate, the better flavor will be achieved.

9. Spray a baking sheet with cooking spray or place a parchment paper. Place the marinated tofu slices on the baking sheet.

10. Bake in a preheated oven at 400 degree F for about 40 minutes or until browned. Flip sides of the tofu in between.

11. Place 2 slices over each of the peanutty quinoa bowls and serve.

Breakfast Tofu and Spinach Scramble with Sweet Cinnamon Quinoa:

Protein per serving: 31 grams

Makes: 4 servings

Ingredients:

For tofu spinach scramble:

- 16 ounces firm tofu, crumbled

- 4 cloves garlic, minced

- 4 cups spinach, chopped

- 1 cup cherry tomatoes, halved

- 1 cup mushrooms, sliced

- Salt to taste

- Pepper powder to taste

- 1/4 teaspoon red chili flakes

- 2 tablespoons soy sauce

- 2 tablespoons lemon juice

For sweet cinnamon quinoa:

- 1/2 cup cooked quinoa

- 2 tablespoons soy milk or almond milk

- 2 handfuls walnuts

- 2 handfuls blueberries

- Stevia to taste or agave nectar to taste

- 1/4 teaspoon ground cinnamon

Instructions:

1. To make Tofu spinach scramble: Place a nonstick pan over medium heat. Add oil to it. When oil is heated, add mushrooms, tomatoes, and garlic. Sauté until the mushrooms are brown and tender.

2. Add tofu, soy sauce, lemon juice, salt and pepper. Heat thoroughly until some moisture is absorbed.

3. Remove from heat and add spinach. Mix well. Cover and keep aside.

4. To make sweet cinnamon quinoa: Add the cooked quinoa to a microwave safe bowl. Add soymilk or almond milk to it. Microwave on high for about 30 seconds. Add walnuts, blueberries, cinnamon and stevia. Mix well.

5. Serve scrambled tofu and spinach with sweet cinnamon quinoa.

Tempeh Hash:

Protein per serving: 20.2 grams

Makes: 6 servings

Ingredients:

- 2 packages tempeh, cut into 1/2 inch size cubes

- 8 medium potatoes, diced

- Water to boil the potatoes

- 1 large onion, diced

- 4 tablespoons soy sauce

- 1 teaspoon garlic powder

- 3 tablespoons olive oil

- Salt to taste

- Pepper powder to taste

Instructions:

1. Place the potatoes in a pot of water. Place the pot over medium heat. Bring to a boil and simmer until the potatoes are tender. Drain and set aside the potatoes.

2. Place a large skillet over medium heat. Add olive oil. When oil is hot, add onions, potatoes and tempeh. Sauté for a couple of minutes and add salt, pepper and

garlic powder. Sauté until the tempeh is well cooked on all the sides.

3. Serve hot.

Breakfast Quinoa with Chocolate and Peanut Butter:

Protein per serving: 31 grams

Makes: 2 large servings

Ingredients:

- 1 cup quinoa

- 3 cups soy milk

- 3 tablespoons cocoa

- 4 tablespoons peanut butter

- 3 tablespoons maple syrup or agave nectar

Instructions:

1. Place a saucepan over medium low heat. Add quinoa and soymilk. Cover and cook until all the milk has been absorbed and quinoa is tender. Stir frequently.

2. Remove from heat. Add peanut butter, cocoa and maple syrup. Mix well and serve immediately.

Gooey Banana Bread Batter Instant Steel Cut Oatmeal

<u>Protein per serving: 12 grams</u>

Makes: 6 servings

Ingredients:

- 1 1/2 cup steel cut oats

- 4 tablespoons chia seeds

- 5 to 6 cups almond milk

- 2 ripe medium sized bananas, mashed

- 2 ripe medium sized bananas, chopped

- A pinch salt

- 1/8 teaspoon nutmeg, grated (optional)

- 1 teaspoon ground cinnamon

- 4 tablespoons pure maple syrup, divided

- 1 1/2 tablespoons vanilla extract

- 4 tablespoons raisins

- 4 tablespoons walnuts, chopped, toasted

- 2 tablespoons dark chocolate, shaved

Instructions:

1. Add oats and chia seeds to a blender and blend to get the texture of flour. Transfer into a heavy bottomed saucepan.

2. Add about 5 cups of almond milk and place the saucepan over medium low heat. Stir constantly. Add mashed bananas, chopped bananas and 2 tablespoons maple syrup. Mix well and heat. Add more milk if necessary.

3. Remove from heat. Add cinnamon, salt, vanilla and nutmeg.

4. Serve in individual bowls. Sprinkle walnuts and raisins. Finally garnish with chocolate shavings.

5. Pour the remaining maple syrup in each of the bowls.

Breakfast Grain Salad:

Protein per serving: 19.3 grams

Makes 4 servings

Instructions:

- 1/2 cup dry golden quinoa

- 1/2 cup dry steel cuts oats

- 1/4 cup dry millet

- 2 1/4 cups water

- 4 teaspoons olive oil

- 1 inch piece ginger, peeled, sliced

- 1/2 cup soy yogurt

- 1/4 cup maple syrup

- Zest of a lemon

- Juice of a lemon

- 1/8 teaspoon nutmeg, grated

- 1/4 cup blueberries

- 1/4 cup blackberries

- 1/4 cup raspberries

- 1/4 cup strawberries, chopped

- 1 cup hazelnuts, chopped, toasted

- 1/4 teaspoon salt or to taste

Instructions:

1. Place oats, quinoa and millet in a fine mesh strainer. Place the strainer under running water. When the water is drained, keep it aside.

2. Place a saucepan over medium high heat. Add 1/2-tablespoon olive oil. Add the rinsed oats mixture to it. Stir-fry for a couple of minutes until they are lightly toasted.

3. Add water, salt, ginger, and half the zest. Mix well and bring to a boil.

4. Lower heat, cover and simmer for about 20 minutes. Remove from heat and let it cool for about 5-7 minutes.

5. Uncover and fluff the grains with a fork. Discard the ginger. Spread the grains on a large plate and let it cool completely.

6. Place the cooled grains in a large serving bowl. Add the remaining zest and mix well.

7. Add remaining olive oil and lemon juice to a bowl and whisk until well combined. Add maple syrup, nutmeg and yogurt. Whisk until smooth. Pour this over the grains and mix well.

8. Add blueberries, strawberries, raspberries, blackberries and hazelnuts. Mix well. Taste and adjust the seasoning if necessary.

9. Refrigerate overnight and serve at breakfast.

Mexican Spiced Tofu:

<u>Protein: 13.9 grams per serving</u>

Makes: 6 servings

Ingredients:

- 3 packages extra firm tofu, drained, pressed, placed on paper towels, chopped into chunks

- 4 scallions, chopped

- 4 cloves garlic, minced

- 1 red bell pepper, chopped

- 1 yellow bell pepper, chopped

- 1 teaspoon Mexican chili powder

- 3/4 teaspoon ground coriander

- 3/4 teaspoon ground cumin

- 1 teaspoon paprika

- 3/4 teaspoon garlic powder

- 3/4 teaspoon dried oregano

- 1 1/2 teaspoons black salt

- 3/4 teaspoon turmeric

- 3 tablespoons nutritional yeast

- 3 tablespoons ground flaxseeds (optional)

- 2 cups water

- 1 1/2 cans (15 ounce each) black beans, drained, rinsed

- 4 tablespoons fresh cilantro, chopped

- 6 ounce canned green chilies

- 2 tablespoons safflower oil or any other vegetable oil of your choice

Instructions:

1. Place a large skillet over medium heat. Add oil. When oil is heated, add scallions, garlic and bell peppers. Sauté until the scallions are translucent.

2. Add tofu and cook until the tofu is browned. Flip sides and cook until brown on all sides.

3. Mix together in a small bowl, chili powder, coriander and cumin powder, paprika, garlic powder, oregano, black salt and turmeric. Sprinkle this mixture over the tofu in the pan and toss well. Add nutritional yeast and toss again. Add flaxseeds if you are using.

4. Mix well. Add about a cup of water and mix well. When the water dries up, add green chilies and black beans. Heat thoroughly. Add cilantro. Mix well and serve hot.

Chapter 5:
Vegan Smoothie and Beverages Recipes

Wake Up Smoothie:

Makes: 6 servings of 1 cup each

Ingredients:

- 2 bananas, peeled, sliced

- 2 1/2 cups orange juice

- 2 1/2 cups frozen berries of your choice

- Sweetener to taste of your choice (optional)

- 1 cup low fat silken tofu

Instructions:

1. Blend together all the ingredients in a blender until smooth.

2. Pour into cups and serve immediately.

Raspberry Avocado Smoothie:

Makes: 4 servings of a cup each

Ingredients:

- 2 avocadoes, peeled, pitted, chopped

- 1 cup frozen raspberries

- 1 1/2 cups orange juice

- 1 1/2 cups raspberries

Instructions:

1. Blend together all the ingredients in a blender until smooth.

2. Pour into cups and serve immediately.

Hot Cocoa:

Ingredients:

- 2 cups cashews, soaked in water for at least an hour

- 2 large medjool dates, pitted, soaked in water along with cashews

- 6 tablespoons pure maple syrup or agave nectar or to taste

- 6 cups water

- 1/2 teaspoon fine grain sea salt or to taste

- 2 ounce dark chocolate

- 1/2 cup cocoa powder

- 2 teaspoons vanilla extract

Instructions:

1. Drain the water from the cashews and rinse well.

2. Blend the cashews, dates, water, maple syrup, cocoa powder, vanilla extract and salt in a blender until smooth and creamy.

3. Transfer into a heavy bottomed saucepan. Add chocolate. Mix well. Place the saucepan over medium heat. The chocolate will melt and get blended with the blended cashew mixture. Stir constantly. When it is hot remove from heat and serve in cups garnished with some chocolate shavings.

4. If you do not like it thick, then add some soymilk or almond milk and thin it according to your liking.

Sesame Banana Milk:

Ingredients:

- 3 medium bananas, peeled, sliced

- 4 cups water

- 1 cup sesame seeds

- 2 teaspoons vanilla extract

- 2 tablespoons maple syrup (optional)

- A pinch of coarse Celtic sea salt

Instructions:

1. Blend together all the ingredients in a blender until smooth.

2. Pour into cups and serve immediately.

Salted Caramel Hot Chocolate:

Ingredients:

- 15 dates, pitted

- 3 cups almond milk

- 3 tablespoons cocoa powder

- 1 1/2 tablespoons corn starch

- Maple syrup to taste

- Coarse Celtic sea salt to taste

- Coconut cream for topping

Instructions:

1. Blend together dates, almond milk, vanilla, cornstarch, cocoa powder a large pinch salt and a little maple syrup in a blender until smooth and creamy.

2. Transfer into a heavy bottomed saucepan. Place the saucepan over medium heat. Stirring constantly let the contents thicken.

3. Pour into mugs. Drizzle a little more of maple syrup. Sprinkle a little salt. Top with coconut cream and serve.

Caramel Vanilla Bean Hazelnut Milk:

Ingredients:

- 1 1/2 cups raw hazelnuts

- 1/2 cup raw almonds

- 5-6 medjool dates or to taste

- 7 cups water

- 2 vanilla beans, chopped

- 1 teaspoon ground cinnamon

- A pinch fine grain sea salt (optional)

Instructions:

1. Soak the almonds and hazelnuts in a bowl of water for at least 8 to 10 hours. Rinse and drain the nuts. If the dates are hard, then soak the dates too.

1. Transfer the nuts into a blender. Add water, dates, vanilla bean, ground cinnamon and salt. Blend the contents until smooth and creamy.

2. Take a nut milk bag and place it over a large bowl. Pour the milk form the blender into the bag. Squeeze the bottom of the bag to strain the milk. Store in masons jars until use.

3. Shake the jars well before use.

4. This milk can last for 3 to 5 days when refrigerated.

Homemade Vanilla Cinnamon Almond Milk:

Ingredients:

- 2 cups raw almonds
- 7 cups filtered water
- 8 medjool dates
- 1/2 teaspoon ground cinnamon
- 2 whole vanilla beans, chopped
- A pinch fine grain sea salt

Instructions:

2. Soak the almonds in a bowl of water for at least 8 to 10 hours. Rinse and drain the nuts. If the dates are hard, then soak the dates too.

3. Transfer the nuts into a blender. Add water, dates, vanilla bean, ground cinnamon and salt. Blend the contents until smooth and creamy.

4. Take a nut milk bag and place it over a large bowl. Pour the milk form the blender into the bag. Squeeze the bottom of the bag to strain the milk. Store in masons jars until use.

5. Shake the jars well before using.

6. This milk can last for 3 to 5 days when refrigerated.

Chapter 6:
Vegan Bakes n Breads

Quick Whole Wheat Bread:

Ingredients:

- 1 1/2 cups whole wheat flour

- 1 1/2 tablespoons sugar

- 1 1/2 teaspoons salt

- 3 1/2 teaspoons active dry yeast

- 1 1/2 cups Luke warm water

- 3 tablespoons extra virgin olive oil

Instructions:

1. To a large mixing bowl, add whole-wheat flour, sugar, salt, and yeast. Mix until well combined.

2. Gently pour olive oil and water. Mix well and knead into dough. Knead for 10 minutes either with your hands or food processor with the dough kneading attachment on low speed.

3. Grease a bowl liberally with some soil. Place the kneaded dough in the bowl. Coat the dough with the oil in the bowl.

4. Cover the bowl loosely and keep aside for 45 minutes or until the dough doubles in size.

5. Remove the dough from the bowl and slightly knead the dough and place on your work area. Use a rolling pin and roll the dough and place in a 10 by 5 inches loaf pan with the seam side down.

6. Cover with a greased plastic wrap loosely and place the loaf pan in a warm place for about 45 minutes for the dough to rise.

7. Bake in a preheated oven at 450 degree F for 10 minutes.

8. Then lower the temperature 350 degree F and bake for 30 minutes.

9. Remove from the oven and place on a wire rack. When the pan is cool enough to handle, loosen the sides of the bread with a blunt knife and remove the bread loaf from the pan and place on the wire rack to cool completely.

10. Cut into slices and serve.

Vegan Banana Almond Bread:

Ingredients:

- 2 tablespoons flax meal
- 6 tablespoons water
- 4 tablespoons canola oil
- 1 cup vanilla flavored soy yogurt
- 6 ripe bananas
- 1 1/3 cups organic sugar
- 1 teaspoon almond extract
- 2 teaspoons vanilla extract
- 4 scoops plant based protein powder
- 2 teaspoons baking soda
- 20 almonds, chopped
- 1 teaspoon salt

Instructions:

1. Mix together in a bowl, flax meal and water to make vegan egg. Set aside for a while.

2. Place bananas in a bowl and mash it with a fork. Add soy yogurt, sugar, canola oil, vanilla extract, and almond extract. Mix well. Add the vegan egg.

3. Mix together in another bowl, flour, protein powder, baking soda and salt. Add this to the bowl of bananas. Mix well.

4. Divide and pour into 2 lightly greased 9-inch loaf pans. Sprinkle almonds on top.

5. Bake in a preheated oven at 350 degree F for about 50 to 60 minutes or until a toothpick when inserted in the center of the bread comes out clean.

6. Remove from the oven and place on a wire rack to cool. Cut into slices and serve.

Hot Dog Pretzel Buns:

Ingredients:

- 3 cups whole wheat flour

- 3 cups unbleached all-purpose flour

- 3 teaspoons garlic, minced

- 3 tablespoons vital wheat gluten (optional)

- 3 1/2 teaspoons active dry yeast

- 3/4 cup water

- 1 1/2 cups soy milk or almond milk

- 1 1/2 tablespoons vegetable oil

- 6 tablespoons maple syrup

- 4 teaspoons baking soda

- 2 teaspoons sea salt

Instructions:

1. Pour water, maple syrup and soymilk to a saucepan. Place the saucepan over medium heat and warm the contents.

2. Transfer the mixture into a large bowl. Sprinkle yeast over it. Set aside for 10 minutes for the yeast to begin frothing.

3. Add the flours, wheat gluten and garlic. Knead to form smooth dough either with your hands or in the food processor with the dough kneading attachment.

4. Divide the dough into 12 equal parts and form balls of it. Cover and set aside for another 15 minutes.

5. After 15 minutes, place the dough on your work area. Dust with a little flour and roll each ball into a cylindrical shape of about 7-8 inches long.

6. Place the buns on a baking sheet. Leave a gap of at least 2 inches while placing the buns on the baking sheet.

7. Cover and let it stand for 30 minutes.

8. Meanwhile boil 8 cups of water in a large pot. Lower heat and baking soda to the water.

9. Add the buns to the boiling water. Cook for 30 seconds per side.

10. Remove and place on a baking sheet, which is lined with parchment paper. Leave a gap of at least an inch while placing the buns. Sprinkle sea salt over it.

11. Make a couple of slits on the top of the buns.

12. Bake in a preheated oven at 425 degree F for 13 minutes.

13. Remove from the oven and cool on a wire rack.

Pita Packets with Broccoli and Tofu:

Ingredients:

For Pit packet covers:

- 1 teaspoon active dry yeast

- 2 1/2 cups warm water

- 2 cups whole wheat flour

- 4 cups all purpose flour

- 1 teaspoon salt

For the filling:

- 2 medium heads broccoli, minced

- 2 packages (12 ounce each) extra firm tofu, drained, crumbled

- 1 large onion, minced

- 3 tablespoons garlic, minced

- 2 teaspoons cumin powder

- 2 tablespoons coriander powder

- 2 teaspoons vegetable oil

- 1 teaspoon cayenne pepper

- Salt to taste

For sautéed greens:

- 12 ounce frozen spinach, thawed

- 12 ounce frozen kale, thawed

- 1 1/2 teaspoons black mustard seeds

- 2 teaspoons vegetable oil

- 2 teaspoons red chili flakes or to taste

- Salt to taste

- Cooking spray

For cilantro chutney:

- 1 cup cilantro leaves, chopped roughly

- 1 green chili

- 1-2 tablespoons water

- 1/4 teaspoon salt

- Juice of a lemon

Instructions:

1. To make pita covers: Pour warm water in a mixing bowl. Water should be warm and not hot.

2. Sprinkle yeast over the water. Leave aside for 5 minutes. Add the whole-wheat flour and a cup of all-purpose flour. Mix well to form loose dough. Leave aside for 15-20 minutes.

3. Add the remaining flour, a little at a time and mix well to get stiff dough. Knead for 5 minutes to get smooth dough.

4. Place the dough in a bowl that is oiled liberally. Coat the dough with the oil of the bowl.

5. Cover with a kitchen towel and place the dough in a warm place for about 2 hours or until the dough has become double in size.

6. When the dough is double in size, knead slightly and divide into 1-inch diameter balls. Roll them into smooth round balls. Cover with kitchen towels and leave it aside for 10-15 minutes.

7. To make the filling: Place a skillet over medium heat. Add oil. When oil is heated, add onions. Sauté until the onions are pink. Add garlic and sauté until the garlic is fragrant.

8. Add cayenne pepper, coriander and cumin powders. Mix well and add broccoli and salt. Cook until the moisture dries up. Add tofu and mix well. Heat thoroughly until all the moisture evaporates. Add salt and remove from the heat, and transfer into a bowl and keep aside

9. To make the sautéed greens: Place the skillet back on heat. Add oil. When oil is heated, add mustard seeds. When the complete spluttering, add red chili flakes, salt, spinach, and kale.

10. Cover and cook until the greens are tender.

11. To make the pita packets: Dust your work area with a little flour. Take a ball of the dough and using a rolling pin, roll the ball into a thin circle of about 5 inches diameter.

12. Place about 2 tablespoons of the filling in one half of the circle. Brush a little water all around the edges of the circle. Fold one half over the other like a calzone.

13. Press the edges of the filled semi circle with a fork to make it stay firm. Place on a greased baking sheet.

14. Repeat steps 11, 12, and 13 with the remaining balls of dough.

15. Spray some cooking spray on the packets and bake in a preheated oven at 450 degree F for about 15 minutes.

16. Remove from the oven and place on a wire rack to cool for about 5 minutes.

17. Meanwhile, prepare the chutney as follows: Blend together all the ingredients of the chutney in a blender. Transfer into a small bowl.

18. Serve hot with cilantro chutney

Garlic Herb Buns:

Ingredients:

- 1 cup whole wheat flour

- 1 cup all purpose flour

- 3/4 cup warm water

- 1/2 tablespoon + 1/2 teaspoon active dry yeast

- 2 tablespoons sugar

- 1/2 teaspoon salt

- 1 egg replacer mixed with a little soy milk

- 1-2 tablespoons sesame seeds

For garlic and herb mix:

- 1/2 tablespoon garlic powder

- 1/2 teaspoon dry rosemary

- 1/2 teaspoon dry thyme

Instructions:

1. Pour warm water in a mixing bowl. Water should be warm and not hot. Add water and sugar. Sprinkle yeast over the water. Leave aside for 5 minutes.

2. Add salt and both the flours. Knead into dough either using your hands or in the food processor with the

dough attachment on low speed. If the dough is too soft, add a little more flour.

3. Place the dough in a bowl that is oiled liberally. Coat the dough with the oil from the bowl. Place the bowl in a warm place for about 45 minutes.

4. Knead the dough slightly. Place the dough on your work surface. Slightly oil the work surface. Using a rolling pin, roll the dough into a rectangle.

5. Mix together all the ingredients for the garlic and herb mix.

6. Spread the garlic herb mixture all over the rolled dough. Starting from one end of the rectangle, roll the dough into a log.

7. Use a sharp knife and chop the log into 1 inch long pieces. Place the pieces on a greased baking sheet. Press each piece into a circle. Place the pieces with a gap of at least 2 inches.

8. Cover it loosely with a plastic sheet or kitchen towel and keep aside for about an hour.

9. Brush the buns with a little of egg replacer. Sprinkle sesame seeds on it.

10. Bake in a preheated oven at 375 degree F for 25 minutes. Remove from the oven and let it cool for 10 minutes.

11. Remove and place on a wire rack to cool completely.

Chia Bread:

Instructions:

- 3/4 cup chia seeds

- 3/4 cup raw sunflower seeds

- 3/4 cup gluten free rolled oats,

- 3/4 cup raw pumpkin seeds

- 6 tablespoons raw buckwheat oats

- 1 1/2 teaspoons sugar

- 1/2 teaspoon garlic powder

- 1/2 teaspoon onion powder

- 1 1/2 teaspoons dried oregano

- 3/4 teaspoon dried thyme

- 1 1/2 cups water

- A little fine grain sea salt

Instructions:

1. Place rolled oats and buck wheat in a high-speed blender and blend until flour of fine texture is got.

2. Transfer into a large mixing bowl. Add all the ingredients except water and mix well.

3. Add water and mix well. The mixture will thicken soon. Line a square pan with 2 pieces of parchment paper. Place the paper such that you can lift the bread by holding the sides of the paper. Transfer the dough into the pan. Spread with a spatula evenly. Sprinkle a little sea salt all over the dough.

4. Bake in a preheated oven at 325 degree F for 25 minutes. Remove from the oven and let it cool in the pan for about. Lift with the parchment paper from the sides and place on the wire rack to cool completely.

5. Slice and serve. It can last for 2 to 3 days.

Vegan Zucchini Bread:

Ingredients:

- 9 tablespoons ground flaxseeds
- 3/4 cup warm water
- 3 cups light brown sugar
- 3/4 cup vegetable oil
- 1 1/2 teaspoons vanilla extract
- 3 cups all purpose flour
- 1 1/2 cups whole wheat flour
- 3/4 cup apple sauce
- 1 1/2 tablespoons baking soda
- 3 1/2 cups zucchini, grated
- 3/4 teaspoon baking soda
- 1 1/2 tablespoons ground cinnamon
- 1 1/2 teaspoons salt
- 3 teaspoons nutmeg
- 1 cup raisins or chocolate chips (optional)

Instructions:

1. Mix together flax seeds and warm water in a mixing bowl. Add oil, sugar, applesauce and vanilla extract. Whisk well.

2. Add zucchini and mix well.

3. Sift all the dry ingredients and add to the zucchini mixture. Mix until well combined.

4. Grease 2 loaf pans. Divide and pour the batter into the pans.

5. Bake in a preheated oven at 350 degree F for about 50-60 minutes or a knife when inserted in the center of the bread comes out clean.

6. Let it cool. Remove the bread from the pan and cool on a wire rack.

7. Slice and serve.

Banana Nut Muffins:

Ingredients:

- 1 cup whole wheat flour

- 2 over ripe bananas

- A pinch salt

- 1 teaspoon vanilla extract

- 6 tablespoons brown sugar

- 2 tablespoons vegan butter

- 2 small vegan flax eggs

- 1/2 cup walnuts

Instructions:

1. Place the bananas in a large bowl and mash it. Add brown sugar, baking soda and salt and whisk.

2. Add flax eggs, vanilla extract, melted vegan butter and mix.

3. Add flour and fold until just combined.

4. Grease 4 ramekins or muffin molds. Divide and pour the batter into the molds.

5. Sprinkle walnuts over it,

6. Bake in a preheated oven at 375 degree F for about 25 to 30 minutes or a toothpick when inserted comes out clean.

7. Remove from the oven and let it cool for a while. Invert on to a plate and remove the muffins and serve warm.

Spiced Carrot Muffins:

Ingredients:

- 1 tablespoon ground flaxseeds
- 1 cup carrots, grated
- 3 tablespoons water
- 1/2 cup rolled oats
- 1 tablespoon rolled oats for topping
- 1 cup all-purpose flour
- 1 teaspoon baking powder
- 1 teaspoon ground cinnamon
- 1/4 teaspoon salt
- 1/4 teaspoon nutmeg
- 1/4 teaspoon ground ginger
- 1/4 cup coconut oil
- 1/2 cup plain almond milk, unsweetened
- 1 teaspoon vanilla extract
- 6 tablespoons brown sugar

Instructions:

1. Mix together flax seeds and warm water in a mixing bowl. Keep it aside

2. Whisk together flour, oats, and baking powder, salt, nutmeg, cinnamon and ground ginger in a large bowl.

3. Pour coconut oil in a microwavable bowl. Microwave for 20 seconds at 50 % power. Remove from the microwave.

4. Add flaxseed mix, carrots, almond milk, brown sugar and vanilla extract. Mix well.

5. Add this mixture to the flour mixture. Stir with a wooden spoon. All the ingredients should just mix. Do not over mix.

6. Grease muffin molds. Pour batter (fill it only up to 1/3) into the muffin molds.

7. Sprinkle 1-tablespoon oats on top.

8. Bake in a preheated oven at 375 degree F for about 15-18 minutes or until a toothpick when inserted in the center comes out clean.

9. Remove from the oven and let it cool for a while. Invert on to a plate and place on a wire rack to cool.

Crispy Quinoa Cakes:

Ingredients:

- 2 1/4 cups cooked quinoa

- 3 tablespoons ground flaxseeds

- 9 tablespoons water

- 3/4 cup rolled oats, ground into flour

- 1 1/2 cups kale, remove hard stems and ribs, chopped

- 3/4 cup sweet potato, grated

- 1/4 cup onions, chopped

- 6 tablespoons fresh basil leaves, finely chopped

- 6 tablespoons sunflower seeds

- 6 tablespoons oil packed sun dried tomatoes, chopped

- 2 cloves garlic, minced

- 1 1/2 tablespoons watery tahini paste

- 2 1/2 teaspoons red or white wine vinegar

- 2 1/2 teaspoons dried oregano

- 3/4 teaspoon fine grain sea salt or to taste

- 4 1/2 tablespoons all-purpose flour

- 1/2 teaspoon red pepper flakes or to taste

Instructions:

1. Mix together flax seeds and warm water in a mixing bowl. Keep it aside.

2. Mix together all the ingredients in a large bowl. Add flaxseed mixture and mix well.

3. Divide the mixture into balls and using your hands, shape into patties. Place the patties on a large lined baking sheet.

4. Bake in a preheated oven at 400 degree F for about 15 minutes. Flip sides and bake for 10 minutes or until golden brown.

5. Serve hot.

Chapter 7:
Vegan Sandwiches and Burger Recipes

Avocado Sandwich with Lemon Basil Mayonnaise:

Ingredients:

- 2/3 cup vegan mayonnaise

- Zest of a lemon, grated

- 2 ripe tomatoes, thinly sliced

- 2 avocadoes, peeled, pitted, thinly sliced

- 16 slices vegan bacon

- 1/4 cup fresh basil, chopped

- 8 slices bread, toasted

- 1 cup broccoli sprouts

- Salt to taste

- Pepper powder to taste

Instructions:

1. Mix together in a bowl, mayonnaise, basil, lemon and pepper.

2. Place the tomato slices over the bread. Layer with avocado slices followed by vegan bacon and broccoli.

3. Top with the mayonnaise mixture and serve immediately.

Tortas and Pambazos (Mexican fried Eggplant Sandwiches):

Ingredients:

- 4 medium poblano peppers

- 2 medium eggplants, cut into 1/2 inch thick rounds

- 1 cup flour

- Salt to taste

- 2 cups refried beans

- 2 cups panko style breadcrumbs

- 4teaspoons dark molasses

- 4 tablespoons chipotle pepper in adobo sauce, finely chopped

- 8 sandwich rolls, halved

- 1 1/2 cups pickled red onions

- 4 cups iceberg lettuce, shredded

- 2 avocadoes, peeled, pitted, sliced

- 2 tablespoons cilantro, chopped

- 3 cups enchilada sauce

- Oil for frying

Instructions:

1. Place the poblano peppers over the gas burner and cook until charred. Place in a bowl and cover with plastic wrap. Set aside.

2. Sprinkle eggplant slices with salt and pepper. Place the slices on a plate that is lined with paper towels. Cover with another paper towel. After a while press the slices to remove any excess moisture.

3. Mix together flour and 1 cup water in a medium bowl. Add salt. Place the panko breadcrumbs in another bowl.

4. Place a large wok over medium heat. Add oil enough to drown the eggplant slices in it.

5. Meanwhile as the oil is being heated, Dip 3 to 4 eggplant slices in the flour mixture. Tap off the excess batter. Dip into the bowl of panko breadcrumbs. Coat well and place on a plate.

6. When the oil is nice and hot, add 3 - 4 slices of eggplants to it. Cook on both sides until golden brown. Remove on to a plate that is lined with paper towels. Sprinkle salt over it.

7. Fry the eggplant slices in batches.

8. Meanwhile peel the charred skin of the poblano peppers. Discard the stems and seeds. Cut into about 1/4 inch strips.

9. Mix together in a bowl, refried beans, chipotle peppers and molasses. Mix well with a fork until well combined.

10. To arrange the sandwiches: Spread the refried bean mixture on the bottom half of the rolls.

11. Lay the pepper strips over it. Place fried eggplants, pickled red onions, and lettuce over it. Sprinkle cilantro. Place the avocado slices over it. Close the sandwiches with the top half of the rolls. Press gently.

12. Serve as it is for tortas or place in a Panini press for a few minutes.

13. To make pambazos: Pour enchilada sauce in a large bowl. Place a sandwich in it so as to dip it. Apply with spoon on the top part of the roll. Remove and place in a Panini press. Grill for 3-4 minutes until the sauce is slightly charred.

14. Serve immediately.

Four Layered Sandwich:

Ingredients:

For pesto:

- 2 cloves garlic

- 2 cups fresh basil leaves

- 1/2 cup sun dried tomatoes (with the oil)

- 1/2 cup hemp seeds

- 1/4 cup water

- 1/4 cup extra virgin olive oil

- 1/4 cup lemon juice

- 1/2 teaspoon salt or taste

- 1/2 cup hemp seeds, hulled

- Black pepper powder to taste

For the sandwich:

- 8 slices sprouted-grain bread, toasted

- 4 tablespoons hummus

- 4 tablespoons sun-dried tomato and hemp basil pesto - recipe given below

- 1 avocado, sliced thinly

- Lettuce leaves

- 4 tomato slices (thin)

- Red pepper flakes (as per taste)

- A pinch of salt

- A pinch of pepper

Instructions:

1. To make pesto: Blend together in a blender all the ingredients of the pesto until smooth.

2. Spread hummus over 4 slices of toasted bread. On the other 4 slices, apply pesto.

3. Place lettuce leaves, tomato, and avocado on any 4 of the slices of bread. Sprinkle red pepper flakes, salt and pepper. Cover with the remaining 4 slices of bread.

Mexican Mushroom and Spinach Sandwich

Ingredients:

- 4 medium poblano peppers
- 20 ounces white button mushrooms, thinly sliced
- 16 ounce fresh spinach leaves
- 4 cloves garlic, finely sliced
- Pepper powder to taste
- Salt to taste
- 2 cups refried beans
- 4teaspoons dark molasses
- 4 tablespoons chipotle pepper in adobo sauce, finely chopped
- 8 sandwich rolls, halved
- 6 whole pickled jalapeno peppers, stems and seeds discarded, cut into thin strips
- 1 cup pickled red onions
- 2 avocadoes, peeled, pitted, sliced
- 2 tablespoons cilantro, chopped
- 4 tablespoons olive oil

Instructions:

1. Place the poblano peppers over the gas burner and cook until charred. Place in a bowl and cover with plastic wrap. Set aside.

2. Place a large saucepan over high heat. Add oil. When oil is hot, add mushrooms, salt and pepper and cook until brown.

3. Add garlic and sauté for a couple of minutes until fragrant. Add spinach and sprinkle a little water. Cook until the spinach wilts and the water dries up. Add salt and pepper. Mix well and remove on to a plate that is lined with paper towels. Keep aside for a while so as to drain out any moisture present.

4. Meanwhile peel the charred skin of the poblano peppers. Discard the stems and seeds. Cut into about 1/4 inch strips.

5. Mix together in a bowl, refried beans, chipotle peppers and molasses. Mix well with a fork until well combined.

6. To arrange the sandwiches: Spread the refried bean mixture on the bottom half of the rolls. Lay the pepper strips over it.

7. Place spinach and mushroom mixture, jalapeno slices, pickled red onions, and cilantro over it. Place the avocado slices over it. Close the sandwiches with the top half of the rolls. Press gently.

8. Serve it as it is or place in a Panini press for a few minutes and serve.

Broccoli Rabe and Antipasti Panini with Olive Salad:

Ingredients:

For olive salad:

- 1 cup mixed Italian olives, pitted, finely chopped

- 4 jarred pepperoncini, stems removed, finely chopped

- 1 cup giardiniera, (Italian pickled vegetables) finely chopped

- 2 teaspoons garlic, grated

- 2 tablespoons capers, drained, chopped

- 1/2 cup extra virgin olive oil

For broccoli rabe:

- 3 pounds broccoli rabe, discard thick stems, chopped

- Pepper powder to taste

- Kosher salt to taste

- 2 cups dry white wine

For assembling the sandwiches:

- 1/2 pound red peppers, roasted

- 1/2 pound sun dried tomatoes, cut into thin strips

- 4 round Italian style loaves (about 8 inches diameter), halved

- 2/3 pound marinated artichoke hearts, cut into 1/4 inch thick slices

Ingredients:

1. For olive salad: Mix together all the ingredients in a bowl. Mix well and set it aside.

2. For broccoli rabe: Place a large skillet over medium heat. Add oil. When oil is heated, add garlic and sauté until light brown. Add broccoli rabe and white wine.

3. Raise the heat to high and stir-fry until broccoli rabe wilts. Lower the heat to medium low and let it simmer until tender. If the moisture dries up, sprinkle some water in it. Sprinkle salt and pepper over it.

4. To arrange the sandwiches: Spread some olive oil salad on both the cut surfaces of the loaf.

5. Place some broccoli rabe, red peppers, artichoke hearts, and sundried tomatoes on the bottom half of each of the bread loaves. Close the sandwiches with the top half of the bread loaves.

6. Serve it as it is or press in a Panini press for a few minutes until grilled and crisp. Cut into desired shapes and serve.

French toast:

Ingredients:

- 9 slices bread preferably thick slices

- 1 ½ cup almond milk or any non-dairy milk of your choice

- 3 tablespoons silken tofu

- 1 ½ tablespoons nutritional yeast

- 1 ½ teaspoons granulated sweetener

- 1 ½ teaspoon vanilla

- ½ teaspoon sea salt

- ¾ teaspoon ground cinnamon

- ¼ teaspoon ground nutmeg

- 1 ripe banana or ½ cup blue berries (optional)

- Canola oil as required

Instructions:

1. Blend together milk, tofu, nutritional yeast, granulated sweetener, vanilla, salt, cinnamon, banana or blueberries if you are using and nutmeg in a blender until smooth.

2. Place a frying pan over medium heat. Add about 1 teaspoon canola oil.

3. Dip a bread slice in the blended tofu mixture. Make sure to cover both the sides. Place it on the frying pan. Cook until the bottom side is golden brown. Flip sides and cook the other side until golden brown.

4. Repeat with the rest of the bread slices. Serve hot with a fruit of your choice

Vegetable and Hummus Sandwich:

Ingredients:

- 1/4 cup hummus
- 4 slices sprouted whole grain bread, toasted
- 6-8 cucumber slices
- 4-6 tomato slices
- 6-8 slices avocado
- 1/2 cup alfalfa sprouts
- 1/2 cup carrots

Instructions:

1. Spread about a tablespoon each of hummus on one side of all the slices of bread.

2. Place cucumber slices over it followed by tomato slices, avocado, sprouts and carrots.

3. Serve immediately.

Spicy Sandwiches:

Ingredients:

- 2 vegan frozen spicy burgers
- 1 red bell pepper, chopped into thin slices
- 1 sweet onion, sliced into rounds
- 1/2 tablespoon olive oil
- 1/2 cup salsa of your choice
- 2 tablespoons nutritional yeast
- Pepper powder to taste
- Salt to taste
- 1/3 cup garlic hummus
- 4 slices sprouted grain bread, toasted
- 2 tablespoons fresh parsley, chopped

Instructions:

1. Place a nonstick pan over medium heat. Add oil. When oil is hot, add onions and bell pepper and sauté until onions are translucent.

2. Add pepper and nutritional yeast. Sauté for a couple of minutes and salsa. Increase the heat to high and sauté the vegetables until the moisture is absorbed.

3. Push the vegetables to one side of the pan. Place the burgers and heat thoroughly. Remove the pan from heat.

4. Apply hummus over the bread slices Spread the sautéed vegetables over 2 of the bread slices. Sprinkle salt and pepper to taste. Place the burger over it. Sprinkle parsley over it. Cover with the remaining 2 slices of bread and serve with hummus.

Swiss Chard & White Bean Sandwich:

Ingredients:

- 10 slices bread

- 5 leaves Swiss chard

- 2 radishes, thinly sliced

- Few tomato slices

- 4 tablespoons vegan butter

- Salt to taste

- Pepper to taste

- 8-10 tablespoons white bean spread

Instructions:

1. Spread about a tablespoon of white bean spread on one side all the slices of bread.

2. Place Swiss chard over 5 slice of bread. Arrange tomato slices over the bread.

3. Next layer the radish slices over the tomatoes. Cover with the remaining bread slices.

4. On the other side of the bread, spread vegan butter lightly.

5. Place a nonstick pan over medium heat. Place the sandwich on the pan and cook until golden brown. Flip sides and cook the other side too.

6. Cut into 2 pieces and serve.

Tofu Club Sandwich:

Ingredients:

- 2 packages tofu, chopped into 5mm slices

- 10-12 slices bread, toasted

- A few lettuce leaves

- 1 avocado, peeled, pitted, sliced

- 1 cup onions, sliced

- 4 cloves garlic, minced

- 1 tablespoon oil

- 2 sprigs of fresh rosemary or 2 teaspoon dried rosemary

- A few fresh basil leaves

- 2 tomatoes, sliced

- A little mustard sauce

- 1/2 cup tahini to spread

- Salt to taste

Instructions:

1. Place a frying pan over medium heat. Add oil. When oil is hot, add onions and garlic. Sauté until the onions are translucent.

2. Add tofu. Fry until golden brown. Flip sides and cook the other side until golden brown. Remove from heat and keep aside.

3. Spread tahini on one side of all the slices of bread.

4. Lay lettuce leaves on 5 slices of bread. Place a little mustard over the lettuce. Lay the tomato slices, avocado and tofu.

5. Lay 3-4 basil leaves and cover with more bread slices to which tahini is applied. Slice into the shape you desire and serve.

Chickpeas Sandwich:

Ingredients:

- 2 cans (19 ounce each) garbanzo beans, drained, rinsed
- 2 stalk celery, chopped
- 1 onion, chopped
- 2-3 tablespoons vegan mayonnaise
- 2 tablespoons lemon juice
- 2 teaspoons dried dill
- Salt to taste
- Pepper powder to taste
- Few bread slices

Instructions:

1. Mash the chickpeas slightly with a fork.

2. Mix together all the ingredients of the filling along with the chickpeas in the bowl. Place the filling in between 2 slices of bread.

3. Serve as it is or grilled. Chop it into the desired shape and serve

4. 1234567890

Corn and Chickpeas Burger:

Ingredients:

- 1 can (19 ounce) chickpeas, drained
- 1 1/2 cups canned sweet corn
- 1/4 cup fresh cilantro leaves, chopped
- 1 teaspoon paprika or to taste
- 1 teaspoon ground coriander
- 1 teaspoon ground cumin
- 1/2 teaspoon lemon zest, grated
- 1/4 cup all-purpose flour
- Salt to taste
- 2-3 tablespoons olive oil
- Few lettuce leaves
- 1 large tomato, chopped into thin slices
- 6 whole meal burger buns, slit
- 1/2 cup ketchup

Instructions:

1. Place chickpeas and sweet corn in the food processor and pulse until crumbly. Add coriander, cumin, salt, lemon zest, flour, paprika and pulse again. Remove the

mixture and divide the mixture into 6 equal portions. Shape into patties. Refrigerate for a while.

2. Place a large frying pan over medium heat. Add olive oil and place the patties in the pan.

3. Cook until the underside is golden brown. Flip sides and cook the other side until golden brown.

4. Apply ketchup at the bottom part of the bun.

5. Place a lettuce leaf on the bottom half of the bun. Place the tomato slices over the lettuce. Sprinkle cilantro.

6. Place fried patty on each of the bun over the cilantro. Cover with the other half of the bun and serve.

Mushroom Burgers:

Ingredients:

- 4-5 tablespoons olive oil

- 2 onions, diced

- 3 cloves garlic, minced

- 5 green onions, sliced

- 1 teaspoon ground cumin

- 3/4 cup diced fresh mushrooms

- 2 cans (15 ounce each) can pinto beans

- 2 teaspoons parsley, chopped

- Salt to taste

- Pepper powder to taste

- A 6 burger buns, slit

- A few slices tomatoes

- A few slices onions

- A few leaves lettuce

Instructions:

1. Place a skillet over medium heat. Add about a tablespoon of oil. Sauté until onions are translucent. Add green onions, cumin, and mushrooms. Cook until the mushrooms are done.

2. Place the beans in a food processor and blend until well mashed.

3. Transfer the contents to a bowl. Add mushrooms, beans, parsley, salt and pepper, Mix well. Divide the mixture into 6 portions and form patties.

4. Place a large frying pan over medium heat. Add a little oil and place the patties in the pan. Cook until the underside is golden brown. Flip sides and cook the other side until golden brown. Place a lettuce leaf on the bottom half of the bun. Place the tomato slices over the lettuce. Place the onion slices over the tomatoes.

5. Place fried patties on each of the bun. Cover with the other half of the bun.

6. Serve with your favorite dip.

Bean Burgers:

Ingredients:

- ¾ cup water

- ½ cup uncooked quick oats

- 1 tablespoon olive oil + more for frying

- 1 onion, finely chopped

- 1 carrot, finely chopped

- 1 tablespoon water

- 2 cloves garlic, minced

- ½ a stalk celery, chopped

- ½ teaspoon basil (dry)

- ½ teaspoon salt

- 1 cup cooked adzuki beans

- 2 tablespoons fresh parsley, chopped

- 6 tablespoons brown rice flour

Instructions:

1. Add ¾ cup water to a saucepan and bring to a boil. Add oats and simmer until thickened.

2. Place a skillet over medium heat. Add olive oil. When the oil is heated, add carrots, onions, celery and garlic. Sauté until the vegetables are tender.

3. Add a tablespoon of water, basil and salt. Cover and cook until dry.

4. Let it cool a bit. Transfer the entire contents into the blender. Add adzuki beans and blend until smooth. Add parsley and pulse for a few seconds. Transfer into a bowl.

5. Add rice flour mixture and mix well. Divide into small balls and flatten to form patties.

6. Place a nonstick skillet. Add about 2 tablespoons olive oil. Add the patties and fry on both the sides until golden brown. Serve hot with a dip of your choice.

Sweet Potato, Chickpea, and Quinoa Veggie Burger:

Ingredients:

- 2 medium sweet potatoes

- 2 cans (15 ounce each) garbanzo beans, rinsed, drained

- 1/2 cup quinoa, cooked according to instructions on the package

- 1/2 cup dry barley, cooked according to instructions on the package

- 1 teaspoon cayenne pepper

- 4 tablespoons parsley

- 3 teaspoons ground cumin

- 1 teaspoon salt or to taste

- 1 teaspoon pepper powder or to taste

- 1/4 cup whole wheat flour

- 1/4 cup olive oil

- 2 red peppers, quartered

- 8 burger buns to serve, slit horizontally

Instructions:

1. Bake the sweet potatoes and red peppers in a preheated oven at 400 degree F. remove the red peppers after 15 minutes and bake the sweet potatoes for about 45 minutes or until cooked. Remove from the oven and cool.

2. Add sweet potatoes, garbanzo beans, parsley, cayenne pepper, cumin, salt, pepper, flour and about 2 tablespoons oil to a food processor. Pulse until you get a crumbly mixture.

3. Transfer into a large bowl. Add cooked quinoa and barley. Mix well.

4. Divide the mixture into 8 portions. Using your hands, form into flat round discs of about 4 inches diameter.

5. Place a nonstick pan over medium heat. Add about a tablespoon of oil. Cook the patties in batches. Cook until the bottom side is brown. Flip sides and cook the other side too.

6. Place the patty between the buns along with a piece of roasted pepper and serve.

Conclusion

Well, there you have it! Fifty of the best and easiest Vegan breakfast recipes that are super-nutritious at the same time. These are not at all cumbersome to prepare and I am sure you would be tempted by now to try out every single recipe here. Just resist the temptation to more than one breakfast a day!

I thank you once again for purchasing this book.

Printed in Great Britain
by Amazon

72262379R00139